SURVIVING PITFALLS ON THE PATH

Surviving Pitfalls On the Path
Copyright © 2018
Beverly ND Clopton

Cover concept and design by David Warren.

All rights reserved. No part of this book may be reproduced, stored in a retrieval system, or transmitted in any form or by any means—electronic, mechanical, photocopy, recording or otherwise—without the prior written permission of the publisher. The only exception is brief quotations for review purposes.

All Scripture quotations are taken from THE HOLY BIBLE, NEW INTERNATIONAL VERSION®, NIV® Copyright © 1973, 1978, 1984, 2011 by Biblica, Inc.™ Used by permission. All rights reserved worldwide.

Published by WordCrafts Press
Cody, Wyoming 82414
www.wordcrafts.net

Surviving Pitfalls on the Path

A 40-Day Devotional for Everyday Believers

BEVERLY ND CLOPTON

WordCrafts

Contents

FOREWORD 1
INTRODUCTION 3
BITTERNESS 6
CHOICES 9
DOUBT 13
WORRY 17
HOPELESSNESS 21
IMPATIENCE 24
HYPOCRISY 28
ANGER 32
FEAR 35
GREED 39
JEALOUSY 43
PRIDE 46
QUARRELING 50
GUILT 53
DESIRES 56
SPEAKER'S REMORSE 60
JUDGMENT 63
LYING 66
SINFULNESS 70
SORROW 73
WORLDLINESS 76
UNFORGIVENESS 79
UNCERTAINTY 83
WEAKNESS 86
TEMPTATION 89
STRESS 92

LONELINESS 96
SUFFERING 99
REVENGE 103
ANXIETY 107
AMBITION 110
COMPLAINING 113
ADDICTION 117
FAILURE 120
PROSPERITY 123
LUST 127
FAVORITISM 131
SELFISHNESS 135
DISAPPOINTMENT 139
CYNICISM 143
A FINAL WORD 147
ACKNOWLEDGEMENTS 150

Foreword

Don't ask what the world needs. Ask what makes you come alive and go do it. Because what the world needs is people who have come alive.
                                        Howard Thurman

Beverly Clopton is a follower of Jesus Christ who has indeed "come alive." Her writing responds to Dr. Thurman's scintillating command to "go do it." In my fifty years of ordained ministry I have not met a person more devoted and disciplined in her study and reflection of God's word than Beverly. Writing for her has become insatiable and compulsive because like Jeremiah there is a "fire shut up in her bones." And it has made her come alive.

Surviving Pitfalls on the Path is Beverly's third book of devotionals. It is a testimony of her own journey on the path. We are all shaped to some extent by our life circumstances. They can make us or break us, inwardly destroy us or make us wounded healers, make us walking zombies or motivate us to come alive. Two particular life circumstances have inexorably shaped Beverly's writing: the sudden death of her husband of thirty years, and the surreal and mysterious brain disorder of her only son that, for now, has rendered him paralyzed and aphasic. These tragedies could have become a spiritual Achilles' heel and plunged her into a pitfall. Instead they have done just the opposite. Rather than sinking into the mire of "why me God," Beverly has chosen to "come alive" through her God-inspired writing.

Beverly pulls from her spiritual trove of experiences and encounters with God as she offers survival strategies for believers who will face pitfalls on their spiritual journey. Most appropriate are the survival teachings offered to readers in search of their heavenly treasure. Readers will also find the selected scriptures compelling and the reflection questions engaging.

We are indebted to this writer for the spiritual acumen she offers in this forty-day devotional. It is a spiritual resource sure to guide the faithful toward the realization of their journey's quest: heaven and its glory.

Rev. Dr. Henry L. Masters Sr.
Publisher, *By Faith Magazine*
Former United Methodist District Superintendent
North Texas Jurisdictional Conference

Introduction

In the path where I walk men have hidden a snare for me.
Psalm 142:3b

Most of us have seen the movies or read the books in which characters in search of hidden treasure fall unsuspectedly into camouflaged traps set by rivals who seek to deter their quest. One moment they're hot on the trail of their perceived destiny, and in the next they are stymied and forced onto a path they had not intended to travel.

In many ways, the Christian journey mimics this scenario. Faithful followers of Jesus are the treasure hunters committed to a path they believe will lead to the ultimate reward: Heaven and all its glory. They've prepared for the trip. They've accepted Jesus as their Savior—the Son of God who died on a cross for their sins and who rose from the grave to defeat death and grant eternal life. They acknowledge one God, the Father who created the world and all therein. They believe in the Holy Spirit and in the Bible as God's inspired word.

But as they set out on the path marked before them, confident they will reach their destination and its rewards, they run into obstacles much like their treasure hunting counterparts.

All too soon they come face-to-face with the enemy of their faith, about whom the apostle Peter writes, *"Your enemy the devil prowls around like a roaring lion looking for someone to devour."* His goal is to take the conditions common to the human experience and use them as snares dotting the path to eternity, and derailing the journey.

Surviving Pitfalls on the Path is a devotional that explores forty snares believers can expect to encounter as they travel the path to their destination. Each chapter exposes the danger of a particular pitfall and offers encouragement and support to help avoid the trap and its entanglements. Both the Old and New Testaments speak to the chapter's pitfall. And as believers turn to their biblical guidebook for help, they come to understand this sacred word is their most powerful ally in defeating the enemy.

> *My eyes are ever on the Lord, for only he will release my feet from the snare.*
>
> Psalm 25:15

To the Reader

You will note that in the early chapters, the *Reflection* section asks you to journal responses to the reflective questions. Even though the later chapters do not specify that you do so, I encourage you to continue journaling. Recording your reflections is a proven strategy for interacting with the text, and I highly recommend it.

He lifted me out of the slimy pit, out of the mud and mire; he set my feet on a rock and gave me a firm place to stand.
                                                            Psalm 40:2

Trust in the Lord with all your heart and lean not on your own understanding; in all your ways acknowledge him, and he will make your paths straight.
                                                            Proverbs 3:5-6

Day 1

BITTERNESS

> *Therefore, I will not keep silent; I will speak out in the anguish of my spirit, I will complain in the bitterness of my soul.*
>
> Job 7:11

Most of us would give Job a pass in his honest exclamation of anguish and Bitterness. We understand his pain and his anger. He's the model man of God. How many of us come anywhere near his piety, about whom the Bible declares, *"This man was blameless and upright; he feared God and shunned evil?"* (Job 1:1) Oh, there may exist a few who approach this level of godliness, but most of us are so far down the ladder we aren't close enough to grasp even the lowest rung.

Because Bitterness resides in the heart, the place reserved for God's spirit, it ranks high on the enemy's pitfall scheme to trap us on the road to glory. The writer of Proverbs cautions there is no joy in a heart filled with Bitterness. (Proverbs 14:10) Precisely for this reason, the Bitterness pitfall is one believers must avoid.

Right about now you're thinking, "I don't know. There

are some things and some people that make me angry and I want to settle the score, or at least get my jabs in. It's not fair when people or life in general bring pain and devastation."

I understand. Even if Bitterness is not your current nemesis, you know of others who are challenged by it. Natural disasters happen unexpectedly and communities are devastated. Lives and homes and livelihoods are lost. Communities are overrun with unrelenting violence; death stalks the streets and there is no haven. Not even the home front is spared the stray bullet or the home invasion perpetrators. Both print and electronic media are filled with stories of sexual exploitation of babies and children; domestic violence; and abuse of power at all levels of our institutions. Loved ones die or suffer devastating illnesses from which the doctors say there is no cure. The list is endless. Though you are a believer, you still fall prey to the feelings of powerlessness these realities present. Even more perplexing sometimes is the reality that your experiences don't typically end as did Job's—restored with more than he had before his losses.

Circumstances such as these represent the soil in which Bitterness takes root. As you travel the path to eternity, if you're not careful, they can grow a spirit of Bitterness. The story of Job is worth another look. He is a prime candidate for what might be termed, "The Bitterness Award of the Year," and though he had reason to, he did not succumb to its budding fruits: self-pity and envy, the seeds that so easily sprout from its pod.

We, on the other hand, though we proclaim Jesus as our Savior, too often embrace these tricks of the enemy when life throws a curve ball we can't field. We feel God has abandoned us. In this state of "woe is me," resentment and blame stealthily commence to order our steps. Blinded by our situation, we don't notice the pitfall ahead on the path. With no warning, the spirit of Bitterness sends us headlong into it.

After thrashing about for some time, seeking to regain our footing, we realize we are no longer in touch or sight of our guide, the Holy Spirit. Thankfully, we remember our biblical guidebook and begin a frantic search for the words that offer rescue. In his letter to the Ephesians, Paul speaks bluntly, *"Get rid of all bitterness, rage and anger..."* Why? A bitter person is full of anger and anger leads to sin. No one traveling the path to glory gets there filled with such a spirit.

The apostle offers further encouragement with the words, *"Be joyful always; pray continually; give thanks in all circumstances, for this is God's will for you in Christ Jesus."* (I Thessalonians 5:16-18) As we allow these words to sink into our spirits, our thoughts return to Job, someone whose experiences might have made him the standard-bearer for Bitterness. Though he questioned God, he did not fall prey to the pitfall. His words provide the balance we need to regain our footing: *"Shall we accept good from God, and not trouble?"* (Job 2:10) Shaken by the encounter, we return to the path, pondering the mishap and wondering what's next?

Reflection

Keep a daily journal of the times when you allow yourself to become bitter. Record the circumstances that led to your feelings. Track yourself for a few weeks and at the end of that time, decide if you are growing in your ability to avoid this pitfall.

Day 2

CHOICES

...then choose for yourselves this day whom you will serve...
But as for me and my household, we will serve the Lord.
Joshua 24:15

Despite crumbled clothing, a few scratches, and a bruised ego, we're thankful to be back on the path. Somewhat sheepishly, we find our place, determined to avoid any future snares. Too quickly, however, we forget how devious the enemy is. His plan, as we round the next bend, is to confound us with confusion; to muddy the waters of the decisions we make and force us off the path again into the next pitfall: Choices.

At first glance it may be hard to think of Choices as a pitfall, something a believer should avoid. But when we recall God's primeval act required Him to make a choice, we get it. God chose to create the world and all therein. Because He created humankind in His image, He gave us that same ability. I think of *choice* as the App God downloaded in His human creation to give it free will, and the subsequent ability to choose to serve Him or not.

Throughout biblical history, making Choices has

confronted people of faith. Moses' admonition to the Israelites in Deuteronomy 30:19-20 resonates still: *"I have set before you life and death, blessings and curses. Now choose life that you and your children may live, and that you may love the Lord your God; listen to His voice, and hold fast to Him."*

What's the popular saying? "The more things change, the more they stay the same." As believers, we certainly concur. Though the lives of these Bronze Age ancestors are different than ours, what remains the same is the human will to either obey God and live, or choose to disobey Him and die. Undoubtedly, the Choices we are required to make daily boggle the mind. But the choice to listen to God's voice as it is recorded in His holy word; to hear His counsel from our contemporary prophets; to feel His prompting in our relationships with our fellow man is no different than what people in every era have experienced.

In the Gospel of John, Jesus himself reminds His listeners, *"You did not choose me, but I chose you and appointed you to go and bear fruit –fruit that will last."* (John 15:16) This lasting fruit is symbolized by the lives of believers who bear witness to who He is by making Choices that honor and glorify Him. In the Gospel of Luke when Martha complained to Jesus that her sister Mary was idling away her time sitting at His feet listening to Him instead of helping with the work that needed to be done, Jesus responded, *"Martha, Martha, you are worried and upset about many things, but only one thing is needed. Mary has chosen what is better, and it will not be taken away from her."* (Luke 10:41-42)

"Ouch," you exclaim. Mary's choice and Jesus' affirmation of it, speak to the importance of intentionally spending time with the Lord—in prayer, meditation, reflection, Bible study, and other devotional exercises. It's a conscious choice the believer makes; not a default one. Developed over time, this practice becomes a habit, and a sure help for avoiding the pitfall and staying on the path.

Think of the multiple Choices you make in the daily routines of life: What time do I get up? Do I have time to pray; to spend some time with my devotionals? Do I give my neighbor a ride? Do I blow my horn and give the universal finger of disrespect to the person who just cut me off as I enter the freeway, or say a prayer that he arrives safely at his destination? Do I watch television or read my Bible? Do I glare in frustration at the minimum wage fast food worker who can't get my order right, or do I smile and say gently, "That's ok?" Do I have time to volunteer this week? Do I cook a healthy dinner for the family or pick up fast food? Do I call my friend, who I know is down in spirits, or put it off to yet another day? Do I text while I'm driving, or listen to inspirational music? Do I reach out to help, even when my own resources are strained?

Choices. On the surface, they seem innocent enough. How can they be considered a pitfall?

As the preacher often says, "I'm glad you asked."

Choices become pitfalls when they take your eyes off the Savior; when they cause you to give short shrift to the faith staples of prayer, Bible study, and reflective quiet time with God; when you elevate the secular at the expense of the sacred; when the choice serves you and not God's purposes; when there is no biblical foundation for the choice; and when try as you might to justify it, the choice conforms to nothing the words of Jesus command of His followers

Reflection

Add to your journaling over the next several weeks the Choices you find yourself making—about mundane things as well as more complex or complicated ones. Take a moment to reflect upon the choice after it's made and done. Did it reflect your understanding of what God desires of His followers? Do you suppose the choice brought a smile or a frown to His face? Was the choice one that secured your steps on the path to glory, or one that sent you plunging into this pitfall? What can you do to avoid this snare of the enemy in the future?

Day 3

Doubt

You of little faith," he said, "why did you doubt?
Matthew 14:31

Our progress has been pretty steady since we confronted Bitterness and Choices, and we escaped their snares. We continue the journey with a little pep in our step. Staying the course, we notice clouds are forming further ahead. As we check our backpack for an umbrella, our cell phone rings. It's someone calling with devastating news. Many of us have received those unexpected calls, and if we haven't, it's because we haven't lived long enough. An accident on the highway has sent someone to the hospital. A parent or spouse has suffered a heart attack, or a child is stricken with a debilitating disease. An act of violence is perpetrated against a relative or friend. Without warning, a house fire destroys everything or a job is terminated without cause. The list is unending. Life circumstances we thought were under control reel away, leaving us frightened, frantic, frenzied. Our steps stagger, and Doubt takes control, pulling us into its lair and off the path.

The dictionary defines Doubt as "uncertainty of belief or

opinion that often interferes with decision making; lack of confidence; an inclination not to believe or accept; distrust." We can see any one of these meanings at play in the biblical moment noted in the chapter scripture. Jesus is speaking to His disciple Peter as he sinks into the sea upon which a moment earlier he had been walking. If you are familiar with the account, you know Jesus was striding on the water toward the boat carrying his disciples. After calming their fears caused by seeing Him, He gives the impetuous Peter leave to step out of the boat onto the water. Scripture doesn't tell us how long he walked; but we know that when Peter noticed the wind, he became afraid and began to sink. As Jesus reached to out his hand to save him, He spoke the words, *"Why did you doubt?"*

We, Peter's biblical descendants, confidently answer that question. Peter doubted because when he took his eyes off Jesus, and looked instead at the winds whipping the waves of the sea, his confidence slipped to zero. More importantly, the situation in which he found himself was precarious enough to allow uncertainty to creep in. His original belief was simple. If Jesus said, *"Come,"* he could do so without question. But in that moment, as belief wavered because the reality of what he was doing was so out of the ordinary, he decided his situation was impossible; that he was drowning, even though the Savior was there, in touching distance. In that moment Peter fell into the pitfall of Doubt; a pitfall now, as it was then, on the path to glory.

Believers determined to claim the prize awarded those who stay the course understand the path will not be level, nor straight; that trials, tribulations, and temptations will be sprinkled upon it like rose petals upon a bridal carpet.

We know we can't be the proverbial Doubting Thomas, the disciple who refused to believe Jesus had risen from the grave unless he could see and touch the wounds in the Savior's hands and side. We cannot allow the dark times that descend and crush our dreams and aspirations to shake our confidence and make us distrust our belief in the Savior's sovereignty. The apostle James instructs us to *"...consider it pure joy when we face trials of many kinds,"* (James 1:2) and he gives a reason for so doing: *"...because the testing of your faith develops perseverance."* (James 1:3)

Perseverance, that ability to hold on and not despair, is exactly the weapon we need to loosen Doubt's grip. We discover, as we persevere through the twists and turns on the path, that our very perseverance helps us keep our focus on Jesus. It is this tunnel vision on the Savior that enables us to wiggle free of the pitfall. What, after all, can free us of unbelief and uncertainty? The surety of Jesus' words alone can counter Doubt and help us to stay the course. He proclaims, *"Have faith in God... I tell you the truth, if anyone says to this mountain, 'Go, throw yourself into the sea,' and does not doubt in his heart but believes what he says will happen, it will be done for him."* (Mark 11:22-23) So it will be for us. Though the path has its pitfalls, we can avoid the one marked Doubt. With our eyes stayed on Jesus, confident that He will not allow us to slip further than His reach, we can cast aside this enemy of our faith and walk steadfastly onward.

Reflection

Record in your journal four or five times when your faith was weakened by a challenge or a tragedy. Did it seem God had forgotten you? Did Doubt creep in and shake your confidence in Him? Did you overcome the Doubt? What helped you regain your trust despite circumstances that might not have changed? Is this pitfall one you still struggle to avoid?

Day 4

Worry

When I said, "My foot is slipping," your love, O Lord, supported me. When anxiety was great within me, your consolation brought joy to my soul.
                                        Psalm 94: 18-19

Of the pitfalls we've encountered so far, perhaps Worry is one of which we should be especially wary. It presents itself as a natural condition of the human DNA. Believers are human after all; how harmful can it really be for them to spend some time wallowing in this pitfall? We must not forget the path to glory is not some country lane, hidden from the world, bordered by fragrant fields, and overshadowed by majestic trees that allow just the right amount of sunshine to light the way—one where we amble leisurely. No, our path stretches before us in hospital hallways leading to the intensive care unit; down congested, noisy, polluted streets that abduct our children and strike down our youth; along the corridors in halls of justice that in too many instances fail to serve those they are sworn to protect; in the aisles of our churches that have forgotten the reason for their existence; in homes filled not with compassion and grace, coated in love, but with fear, violence, and neglect dressed in public personas—conditions ripe for the snare of Worry.

The enemy knows our frailties. What is our first response when we get a call that summons us to the bedside of a loved one who has been rushed to the hospital? Usually we pray all the way there. But the reality is, too many believers link prayer and Worry in a sort of love knot; in effect hoping to tie up all the loose ends of the crisis underway. We sit bedside and our thoughts race: "God, we need You right now in this hospital room. Guide the hands of the doctors and bring your healing touch to my loved one. In Jesus' name, I pray. Amen. OMG, what about the children? What am I going to tell them? What if we don't have enough insurance to cover these expenses? We don't have money in our account if he's out of work too long. Lord, Lord. What are we going to do?" Anxiety grows and though we've read and recited Isaiah 41:10 many times —*"So do not fear, for I am with you; do not be dismayed, for I am your God. I will strengthen you and help you."*—Worry wraps its tentacles around us and we fall.

The human condition is a hotbed that easily grows worry-weeds. We see the kids off to school and then Worry about their well-being on the playground—*will they be bullied*; in the classroom—*will they do well on the test*; in the restroom—*will some pervert attack them*; on the school bus—*will the bus be involved in an accident?* We sit behind the defense table in support of a dear friend on trial, both praying silently for her to be found innocent and at the same time worrying if she can even get a fair trial with the acknowledged biased judge and a jury not made up of her peers. We sit in Sunday worship listening for a word of comfort and peace from the

Lord while worrying at the same time if that business meeting tomorrow will go in our favor or not; worried that if it goes south we won't have the funds to outfit the kids for the new school year. We pray silently for peace and harmony as we gather around the dinner table; at the same time anxious that someone will rouse anger with an ill-spoken word.

In these and any number of scenarios like them, Worry is a menace. In addition, it has the capacity to produce doubt and bitterness; and it certainty affects the choices we make. Though cloaked in the seemingly innocuousness of the "human condition," Worry is not an indulgence we can casually brush aside.

Jesus' take on this pitfall is clear. In chapter six of the Gospel of Matthew, He devotes nine verses of His teachings to the subject. *"Therefore, I tell you, do not worry about your life, what you will eat or drink; or about your body, what you will wear... Who of you by worrying can add a single hour to his life? And why do you worry about clothes? Therefore, do not worry about tomorrow, for tomorrow will worry about itself..."*

Jesus knew this aspect of our human nature is easily shaken; that we are sucked into Worry's tendrils most often when the path we walk is clouded by life's debris. Worry weakens the very faith we depend upon to get us past the enemy's attacks. Some say Worry is a sin because it rejects the teachings of our faith. Paul exhorts in Philippians 4:6, *"Do not be anxious about anything, but in everything, by prayer and petition, with thanksgiving, present your requests to God. And the peace of God, which transcends all understanding, will guard your hearts and minds in Christ Jesus."* The writer of Hebrews reminds us of God's promise that says, *"Never will I leave you; never will I forsake you.* (Hebrews 13:5) And the Apostle Peter reminds us to cast all our anxiety onto Jesus because He cares for us. (I Peter 5:7)

Believers must guard their steps when the Worry pitfall appears on the path. Perhaps a moment's rest on the boulder of faith just there to the left is a good place to pause, grab that Bible out of the backpack, and map a plan of attack. Though the Worry pitfall is alluring, it's siren song having snared many at this juncture, the weapons of prayer and biblical teachings will steer believers over and beyond it.

Reflection

Are you a Worry wart? Do life's ups and downs send you into full-blown Worry mode? In your journal, make a list of the things about which you are most prone to Worry. What strategies can you assign to each that can grow into habits that will enable you to avoid this pitfall? Keep a record of your mastery of this tendency to become anxious and worried. Celebrate and share your success each time you avoid the pitfall.

Day 5

Hopelessness

Why are you downcast, O my soul? Why so disturbed within me?

Psalm 42:5

Empowered once again by the word of God that guides us on this journey to eternity, we purposely secure it within easy reach in the front pocket of the backpack, and stride forward. Eyes even more focused on the road ahead, we muse a moment over the tumble we just avoided; wearisome Worry almost had us. As its haze clears, we eventually turn our thoughts to other things. In that same moment, the enemy, who prowls constantly on the perimeter of our lives in his efforts to destroy us, prepares yet another pitfall on the path.

As Christians, we know the meaning of hope. It is the foundation for our very beliefs. We know it from 1 Corinthians 13, *"Now these three remain: faith, hope and love."* Throughout both the Old and New Testaments we are called to and expected to put our hope in God. These teachings that encourage us to hope are deliberate and timeless; they are needed for the times when, despite our best efforts, we fall prey to a spirit of Hopelessness. The risk of sinking into this pitfall is easy because life circumstances can produce feelings of despair, despondency, and desperation; situations arise that we feel incapable of resolving or redeeming, and when they do, we slip into Hopelessness.

With just a cursory view of the latest newspaper headlines or the red banner scrolling at the bottom of the television screen, we understand the words of the prophet Isaiah when he writes God's message to the Israelites, *"For a moment I abandoned you…"* (Isaiah 54:7). It feels to us as if indeed God has abandoned us. How else can we explain the senselessness of the recent murder-suicide in an elementary school classroom or any of the more recent mass shootings that have claimed the lives of the innocent or unsuspecting? Such repeated incidents speak to the sin that pervades society. Has goodness departed the world? Are we lost in an ever-increasing spiral of violence and depravity? Our feelings of helplessness grow; we despair. We draw nearer the pit.

Even if we manage to avoid the desperation snare by constant prayer and sheer will, we remain targets for despondency. Rejected job resumes, failed relationships, insufficient resources to adequately provide for loved ones, sudden and debilitating illness, death strikes when least expected—life circumstances that produce despondent spirits; situations that pull us off the path and into the pit. As our steps falter and we feel the path give way, what can we grasp to stay the course?

Before we manage even to open our biblical guidebook, the ending words of Isaiah in the passage noted above spring to mind. *"…but with deep compassion I will bring you back."* Yes, God has promised to bring us back from the exile of our despondency and our despair. His words of reassurance and of hope abound. As we turn the pages of our Bible, our eyes fix on these sacred words, bringing the strength we need to pull our feet free from the enemy's snare. As if the very angels are singing from heaven, we read:

"Even youths grow weary, and young men stumble and fall; but those who hope in the Lord will renew their strength. They will soar on wings like eagles; they will run and not grow weary, they will walk and not be faint." (Isaiah 40:31-32)

"Find rest, O my soul, in God alone; my hope comes from him. He alone is my rock and my salvation; he is my fortress; I will not be shaken." (Psalm 62:5-6)

"We have this hope as an anchor for the soul, firm and secure." (Hebrews 6:19)

These reminders, these morsels of hope written to fill the hollows of helplessness that can so easily pull us off the path, inspire us to hold on no matter our circumstances. The words of Job push to the front of our memories: *"...though he slay me, yet I will hope in him."* If we can but muster a measure of that kind of hope, we can avoid this pitfall. Indeed, as the apostle Paul writes, *"What, then, shall we say in response to this? If God is for us, who can be against us?"* (Romans 8:31)

Reflection

Take a moment to reflect upon the seasons of your life when you fell prey to a spirit of helplessness and despair. Record them in your journal. How long did each season last? How did you recover from it? What lessons did you learn that might help others avoid this pitfall? When current circumstances threaten to send you back to this snare, how do you prevent that from occurring?

Day 6

IMPATIENCE

> *Be still before the Lord and wait patiently for him... do not fret—it leads only to evil.*
>
> Psalms 37:7,9

The words of an old spiritual spring to mind about now: *"Nobody told me the road would be easy..."* The refrain speaks to us as we glance back at yet another pitfall we've overcome. With each step forward, it's becoming clearer the path we've chosen to take will not follow a straight line to heaven. No, it's more akin to the life experiences described by the mother in Langston Hughes' poem, *"Mother to Son."* In the dialect of her day, she declares the difficulties she has encountered on life's journey; that it has not been a bed of roses, but rather one in which obstacles she likens to tacks and splinters and torn boards were strewn upon the path she traveled.

This path we're on is like that; its tacks and splinters and torn up boards will take the form of the many twists and turns we encounter. It will try our patience and make waiting on God when He seems to be taking forever or when the going gets rugged, hard to do. Taking matters into our own hands will seem a more logical course to take; not in disrespect, just perhaps to get the ball rolling sooner than later. Just as we embrace this thought, behold, we approach the enemy's next pitfall: the spirit of Impatience.

The psalmist, David, offers us the best advice to avoid this pitfall when he writes, *"Wait for the Lord; be strong and take heart and wait for the Lord."* (Psalm 27:14) In this one verse he employs the word *"wait"* two times; clearly, he wants us to grasp the significance of not being anxious with God's delays; of not becoming irritated or overly desirous when what we want doesn't even seem to be on God's radar.

Recall the saga of Impatience gone awry in the biblical equivalent of a modern-day soap opera: the story of Abram, Sarai, Hagar, Ishmael, and Isaac. Though God had promised Abram he would have an offspring born to him, Sarai became impatient as their years advanced and the promise did not materialize. Since to her it seemed God had forgotten His promise, she decided to take matters into her own hands. She had her husband sleep with her maidservant to produce the child she could not have. The solution was not a positive one. It served only to create friction, anger, jealousy, and abandonment. Had they waited on God to act on His promise of an heir born to them, perhaps the enmity that survives to this day between the descendants of Ishmael and the descendants of Isaac might have been avoided. If only Sarai had not been trapped by the snare of Impatience.

How often are we like Sarai? Eager to find solutions to issues, we devise our own plans, sometimes with a measure of success, but more than we care to admit, with results we regret. What about the times we give up on God because He doesn't seem to hear our pleas? Our loved ones lie in hospital beds unresponsive to the doctor's efforts; our wayward children continue to live dissolute lives despite our prayers; the job does not materialize, though we've submitted hundreds of resumes and worn our best suit to more interviews than we can count. Indeed, not only are these times that try our souls; they are the very soil in which Impatience thrives.

An impatient spirit gets in God's way. It creates anxiety and impulsiveness. Like the effect of the sun's burning rays upon plastic, it warps our attitude and sends us to a rush to judgement. Its counter-virtue, patience, is its only antidote; the only attribute powerful enough to block this attempt of the enemy to lead us off the path. Scripture instructs us to be patient in affliction (Romans 12:12), to wait patiently for the Lord (Psalm 40:1), and to recognize patience as one of the fruits of the Spirit (Galatians 5:22). It was a lesson of the role of patience on life's journey that the mother spoke to in Hughes 'poem. Through all the difficulties life presented, she patiently stayed the course and kept climbing.

We identify with this mother. The path we've chosen to walk is no smoothly paved, straight road. It twists and turns, runs through briar patches, rises to steep inclines and sections cloaked in the darkness of rain clouds. But we who have claimed eternity as our destination will not be snared by any of the enemy's attempts to make us abandon the journey. Our GPS system may falter, but in faith we press onward; and when Impatience's pit opens, by God's grace our spirit of patience will be sufficient to send us sailing above its grasp.

Reflection

Spend some considerable time thinking about what drives you to Impatience: Relationships? Secular concerns? Unanswered prayer? What makes you give up on God and attempt to solve your own problems? Are you quick to say, "God, I need patience, and I need it now?" Set a trial period of four weeks in which you record every incident of Impatience. After that time, look back and ask yourself how you might have avoided the lapses.

Day 7

Hypocrisy

I do not sit with deceitful men, nor do I consort with hypocrites.

Psalm 26:4

In the distance, the road appears to level out. Hopefully that means we are past the snares of the enemy that have marked the journey so far. If but for a few more seasons we could follow the Master, free of entanglements. What a joy that would be. Relieved that we have won the victories over the pitfalls we've left behind, we return to the path, determined to stay the course.

The psalmist David writes our chapter verse. The full psalm speaks of his relationship with God; and in this verse, he offers evidence of his faithfulness. Why, we wonder, was it important for him to declare that he has nothing to do with deceitful, hypocritical men? After all, there are other God-dishonoring behaviors we might consider more serious: jealousy, murder, adultery, and stealing, for example, surely trump deceit and Hypocrisy. As these musings preoccupy us, the enemy seizes the opportunity such reflection offers and does what he does best: he prepares the next pitfall—Hypocrisy.

The dictionary defines Hypocrisy as "pretending to be what one is not or to believe what one does not, especially the false assumption of an appearance of virtue or religion." Both the Old and New Testaments speak to such a character or personality trait as being outside God's design and expectation for those who claim to be His followers. The Book of Isaiah opens with God's proclamation of His displeasure with the people of Israel. He is offended by their outward show of obedience with their temple sacrifices while they persisted in their evil lifestyles. God saw clearly their deeds did not match their hearts, as their disobedience gave evidence. That Hypocrisy is outside God's will is unquestionable. In the seventh chapter of the Old Testament book of Zechariah, He bluntly asks, *"...when you fasted and mourned... was it really for me that you fasted? And when you were eating and drinking, were you not just feasting for yourselves?"*

Jesus says, *"Blessed are the pure in heart for they shall see God."* (Matthew 5:8) During the season of Lent, with its tradition of sacrificial fasting, how many of us can honestly say we observe this Christian rite purely to honor God? Is our abstinence from sweets or meat for more practical reasons, perhaps to drop those clinging ten pounds? Was whatever we "gave up for Lent" for God or for ourselves? Furthermore, whenever as a Christian community we come together with food and drink in fellowship, in all honesty, do we do it to honor God, or just to pleasure ourselves? We cross the line into Hypocrisy whenever we represent our actions as being about serving God when they are in truth only self-serving.

Even when on the surface it appears we are about the Master's business, we must be alert to the enemy's Hypocrisy snare. Note Jesus' words in Matthew 6:2-4: *"For when you give to the needy, do not announce it with trumpets, as the hypocrites do in the synagogues and on the streets, to be honored by men…"* As followers of Christ, we are called to do virtuous deeds without calling attention to ourselves in the execution of them; and we surely are not to expect honor or exaltation. Even when we go to God in prayer, Jesus tells us not to be hypocritical. We don't pray to impress listeners with our intellect, our word mastery, or our biblical knowledge. When we do, we are nothing more than wallowers in the Hypocrisy pitfall. Prayers offered to impress men are not the prayers of the pure in heart.

This issue of Hypocrisy so resonated with the Savior that he condemns repeatedly those who practice it in His teachings in the twenty third chapter of the Gospel of Matthew. In six different examples, He rebukes hypocritical behaviors, pretense, falsehoods, and outward appearances that are not matched by actions.

If Hypocrisy is such an anathema to Jesus, we cannot count it lightly and must at all cost heed His warnings to avoid it. We cannot hypocritically judge others when we ourselves are imperfect—*"Why do you look at the speck in your brother's eye and pay no attention to the log in your own eye? You, hypocrite, first take the log out of your own eye, and then you will see clearly to remove the speck from your brother's eye."* (Matthew 7:3-5) We cannot listen to the word of God, and then hypocritically go our own way, not doing what it says. (James 1:22) Though to the unwary it may seem not all that important, the pitfall of Hypocrisy ranks third in the listing of those things the Apostle Peter says we are to get rid of if we are to be holy. (1 Peter 2:1) Holiness is what we seek on this path leading to eternity.

Reflection

What comes to mind for you personally when you reflect upon the sin of Hypocrisy? Is Hypocrisy really such a big deal? Have you witnessed it in your church or friendship circles? Can you say in all honesty that it is not a sin of which you have been guilty? If you cannot, and can identify times in your life when you came under Hypocrisy's spell, what pulled you away and back into right relationship with the Lord? Record your responses in your journal. Share as you are so led.

Day 8

Anger

In your anger do not sin.

Psalm 4:4

One thing is increasingly clear as we make our way forward, striving to stay the course; this path to eternity is not for the faint-hearted. Our last pitfall was so shrouded in seeming innocuousness that we almost lost our footing and fell prey. But by God's grace, we gleaned the truth just in time.

Moving now at a steady clip, on the lookout for the next potential snare, our attention is drawn to the travelers just ahead of us. Their passionate discussion seems to have escalated; as we observe the increasing tension between them, we are reminded that we live in an angry world. Whether individual or corporate, in large measure, Anger paints the backdrop of the tapestry of our times. We know from our biblical guide book that its manifestation can lead to sin. Sin leads away from the path to glory.

The Apostle Paul writes in his epistle to the Ephesians that believers must not *"let the sun go down while you are still angry, and do not give the devil a foothold."* (Ephesians 4:26) Anger that simmers can give rise to actions that open the door for the enemy's designs. Our first recorded murder was conceived in the heart of an angry man. *"So Cain was very angry, and his face was downcast."* (Genesis 4:5) As you recall, Cain's Anger was in reaction to God's divine action of receiving his brother Abel's offering and rejecting his. He failed to understand the concept of God's sovereignty; even after God asked him point blank, *"Why are you angry? Why is your face downcast? …sin is crouching at your door; it desires to have you, but you must master it."* (Genesis 4:6-7) Cain's Anger turned into sin, the murder of his brother.

At this point it is important to draw a distinction between Anger as a pitfall on our path and what is often called "righteous Anger." Anger that snares the believer creates animosity, rage, fury, and wrath. And these emotions too often lead to vengeful acts, revenge, destruction, or psychological madness. On the other hand, "righteous Anger" is a mindset that seeks constructive ways to address societal injustices perpetrated when the words, "wrong forever on the throne," ring true.

The Anger snare goes beyond annoyance. We all get annoyed by one thing or another; but believers do not allow the mundane irritants of life to simmer or boil over into attitudes or behaviors that lead to sin. Even though there is no specific mention of Anger in the Ten Commandments, there are its by-products: murder, adultery, stealing, false testimony, and covetousness. At the core of each of these prohibitions is the feeling we label, Anger. Surely that is why God warned Cain to not succumb to its influence. He knew that unchecked Anger would cause Cain to sin.

It's no different for today's believer. We secure our steps on this path we trod when we resist Anger and put into practice the words from our biblical resource. *"A gentle answer turns away wrath, but a harsh word stirs up anger."* (Proverbs 15:1) Believers refuse to engage in the tit-for-tat to get in the last word and thereby raise the tension level. *"A fool gives full vent to his anger but a wise man keeps himself under control."* (Proverbs 29:11) Believers express their opinions without losing their cool, thereby sealing the opening for sinful responses.

Finally, believers recall and hold on to the words of the Apostle James when he encourages us to *"be quick to listen, slow to speak and slow to become angry, for man's anger does not bring about the righteous life that God desires."* (James 1:19-20) This is the goal as we traverse this path to heaven—to lead a righteous life that is pleasing to God. When we do, we will easily step around the Anger pitfall.

Reflection

What pushes your button to the Anger level? Is it "righteous Anger," or Anger that leads to sin? Reflect upon the last time you really lost your cool and gave in to Anger. What was the after affect?

Day 9

Fear

Even though I walk through the valley of the shadow of death, I will fear no evil, for you are with me; your rod and staff, they comfort me.

Psalm 23:4

We shake off the dust surrounding Anger's pit, and gain our balance just as the path begins an incline. As the incline increases, the light above us fades. The wind picks up, dark clouds gather, and we wonder if a storm is approaching. Picking up our pace, we fight a growing sensation that perhaps this sudden weather change signals a pitfall just ahead. A nagging sense of dread creeps over us as we move forward.

It's important at this juncture to clarify the term, Fear. For believers, Fear that is synonymous with the profound reverence and awe we manifest toward God is not a pitfall. No, the Fear of the pitfall is unholy Fear, generated by the enemy to stifle our trust in God. It is Fear whose origin can be traced to sin and distrust in God; it has plagued mankind since the beginning of creation. Consider the Bible's account of Adam's reaction in the garden as recorded in Genesis 3:8-10 when God called to him, *"Where are you?"* Adam responded, *"I heard you in the garden, and I was afraid because I was naked; so, I hid."* His nakedness revealed by his sin of disobedience created the first biblical reference to Fear as a pitfall. The Fear Adam felt because of his actions changed the path God had intended for His creation.

Fear generated by disobedience is common to the human experience; perhaps that is why it is such an easy pitfall in which to tumble. Abram, fearful that he would be killed if the Egyptians thought Sarai was his wife, told her to lie and say she was his sister. That deliberate falsehood produced by the terror of death sent Abram sprawling into the Fear snare. In yet another example in ancient biblical history, the patriarch Jacob in his younger years tricked his brother Esau out of his birthright; this disobedient act of trickery caused Jacob to flee in Fear to a distant land to avoid his brother's threat to kill him. Like Abram, Jacob fell into Fear's pit. Even the great King David demonstrated what Fear that sprouts from sin looks like. Fearful that his sin of adultery with Bathsheba would be discovered when she became pregnant, he devised a scheme that insured her husband would be killed in battle. Fear generated by sin pushed David into the pit.

And though disobedience (sin) still causes Fear today, the more common culprit is distrust; distrust of God and His promises despite what His word teaches and what we claim we believe as His followers. If something as benign as a darkening sky and rising winds produce trepidation, it's no wonder that we are prime targets for this snare. The psalmist assures us that *"God is our refuge and strength, an ever-present help in trouble. Therefore we will not fear, though the earth gives way and the mountains fall into the sea…"* (Psalm 46:1-2) Yet, how quickly we panic when situations in our life spiral out of our control or fall apart leaving us teetering on the brink of disaster? Instead of trusting that God is still in control as Psalm 112:7 instructs— *"He will have no fear of bad news; his heart is steadfast, trusting in the Lord..."*—we trip right on over into the pitfall of Fear, just as the enemy desires.

Distrust in God's sovereignty over every aspect of our lives is the sin that snares every time. Jesus was clear that in this world we will have trouble; but He reminded us that He overcame the world, and in so doing assured our victory to do the same. Translation for believers: there is no reason for Fear. Whether we are in a season of health challenges, financial scrimmages, relationship plunges, career assaults, or any of the myriad conditions common to the human experience, God says to us, *"Do not fear, for I am with you; do not be dismayed for I am your God. I will strengthen you and help you; I will uphold you with my righteous right hand."* (Isaiah 41:10)

We can liken our walk on the path to glory to that of Joshua and the Israelites during the Bronze Age as they journeyed to the Promised Land. We are to *"be strong and courageous."* We are not to be *"afraid or terrified"* because of what threatens us or seeks our destruction. The God of Joshua and the Israelites is the same God we serve. Because His word stands forever, it is the same today as it was then: *He will never leave us or forsake us.* (Deuteronomy 31:6) As we stride confidently around the gapping pit of Fear, we say aloud to the enemy therein, *"What, then, shall we say in response to this? If God is for us, who can be against us?"* (Romans 8:31)

Reflection

Meditate for a moment on the Fears you have faced in

the past and perhaps still face now. What have you dreaded most? How did you overcome? What sustains you now and keeps you free of this pitfall?

Day 10

GREED

But among you there must not be even a hint of ... greed.
Ephesians 5:3

The path curves as we leave the last pitfall behind. In a reflective mode, we realize how impossible this journey would be if not for our guidebook, God's Word. As it saved us from the last snare, we are confident of its power to do the same as we approach the next: Greed.

Greed's deceptiveness is its ability to masquerade as someone else's issue. It is the proverbial speck in the other's eye to which we point. We associate its concept of avarice and excessive acquisition with those in high-rise corporate offices; to those whose positions of power are undergirded by their great wealth. Consider as an example the story of King Ahab in 1 Kings 21:1-21. Despite his wealth, the king coveted his neighbor's vineyard that was close to the palace. He wanted the land to plant a vegetable garden. When the owner refused to sell it, both the king and his wife Jezebel were furious; so furious that the queen devised and carried out a plan to kill Naboth. When the deed was done, King Ahab took possession of the property. Seizing the land was an abuse of power fueled by covetous Greed. His action clearly violated the Lord's tenth commandment that forbids coveting anything that belongs to your neighbor. Proverbs 15:27 instructs, *"A greedy man brings trouble to his family."* King Ahab learned firsthand the truth of this teaching. Following his crime, God instructed the prophet Elijah to say to the king, *"Have you not murdered a man and seized his property? In the place where the dogs have licked up Naboth's blood, dogs will lick up your blood—yes, yours!"* And God wasn't done. *"I am going to bring disaster on you. I will consume your descendants...Dogs will devour Jezebel by the wall of Jezreel."* (I Kings 21:19-23)

Now it's easy for us to point the finger in stories like this, or at those in our own time who perpetrate schemes and plans to acquire what others have, and denounce their Greed. Yes, stories of corporate takeovers that cut jobs and benefits to increase profits for those at the top, and gentrification of properties in deteriorated urban neighborhoods by upper-income families that displace low-income families and small businesses are ones that typify the snare of Greed. But calling out the "speck in the eye" in these scenarios does not shield us from the more common practices of Greed to which many of us fall prey. If we are not vigilant on this path to eternity, we can succumb easily to Greed's pull. We too often mimic the man in Luke 12:13-21 who had so much he had to build larger storage facilities to house his possessions. Jesus cautioned against such excessive acquisition with these words, *"Watch out! Be on your guard against all kinds of greed; a man's life does not consist in the abundance of his possessions."*

Is it not Greed that prompts us to rent storage units to house things we've acquired and have no room for any longer in our homes? Is it not Greed that accounts for the shoe boxes piled to the top of the closet, spilling over onto the floor with each new purchase? Is it not Greed that says we must add yet another handbag to the collection that fills the nooks and crannies of the wardrobe area? Is it not Greed that demands we acquire the latest in electronic technology no matter the cost? Is it not Greed that accounts for the bags of clothing castoffs we are continuously giving away because we have no more room for them in the drawers or on the shelves, or because we've just grown tired of the same old look? After all, how many jackets and coats do we need to stay warm? How many pairs of shoes and boots do we need to cover our feet? How many changes of outfits do we really need to cover our bodies? How many televisions per household are enough? Must every room be cable ready?

Yes, these practices of Greed more common to the human experience are no less avaricious than those of the corporate world. Greed is Greed. We avoid it by remembering the counsel of the writer of Ecclesiastes. After he had toiled, denied himself nothing he desired, and achieved all he set out to achieve, he realized that in the end it had no lasting meaning. That, fellow traveler, is why we shake off the lure of Greed, and with great care step over its silent pitfall. In the final analysis, it will not propel us on the journey to heaven. The words of Jesus in His sermon on a mountainside make it clear that a spirit of Greed does just the opposite: *"Do not store up for yourselves treasures on earth, but treasures in heaven. For where your treasure is, there your heart will be also… You cannot serve both God and money."* (Matthew 6:17-24—Paraphrased)

Reflection

Let's be honest. Do you think of yourself as greedy or

avaricious? Do you have a storage unit? What's in it? Have you ever counted the pairs of shoes and handbags you own? When did you last purge your closet(s) to donate your excess to a worthy cause? Reflect upon this pitfall. Do you agree or disagree that individual greediness is comparable to corporate or governmental greediness? Are there steps you can take to reduce the influence of this pitfall in your personal life? Will you covenant to take them?

Day 11

Jealousy

And from that time on Saul kept a jealous eye on David.
1 Samuel 18:9

After the last encounter with the enemy and his snare that momentarily blinded us, we understand more clearly that this path to eternity is not intended to be easy. And why should it? Did not our Savior give His life for our salvation? Should not our commitment to Him require our faithfulness to His teachings? If we continue the journey with this mindset, we can walk the path knowing that another snare is on it; and anticipating that God will enable us to overcome it. Thus grounded, we walk onward.

Our chapter scripture references one of several biblical accounts of how a spirit of Jealousy corrupts the nature God designed for humankind. King Saul grew angry when the people sang of David's victories on the battlefield with the words, *"Saul has slain his thousands, and David his tens of thousands."* (1 Samuel 18:7) This unfavorable comparison angered Saul and made him think perhaps David would take over his kingdom. From anger and negative projections grew a spirit of Jealousy that propelled Saul to murderous actions against David. Even before this time of Israelite kings, the snare of Jealousy brought destruction to the biblical ancestors who succumbed to it. Recall what led to the first account of murder: Cain's Jealousy of his brother Abel (Genesis 4:3-8). Consider how Jealousy was at the heart of the estrangement that cropped up between Moses and his sister and brother, Miriam and Aaron, after Moses led the people out of captivity in Egypt (Numbers 12:1-2).

Jealousy, the "green-eyed monster," challenges us and has the potential, if not checked, to lead us off the path we've chosen to follow. Merriam-Webster's Collegiate Dictionary defines Jealousy as hostility toward a rival or one believed to enjoy an advantage (Saul/David); begrudging (Cain/Abel); resentfulness (Miriam/Aaron); enviousness, spite, resentment, and envy. Now we may not have yielded to its influence to the degree that the aforementioned did, but few of us can say we haven't known this negative emotion at one time or another. If we are honest, we can own the times when we allowed it free rein of our emotions and reactions. We know we shouldn't feel any twinge of Jealousy when others outpace us in our professional or personal lives, but there have been times when that occurred. We know we are not to judge our children's accomplishments against others, nor feel envious if someone else's child outperforms ours, but there have been times when we did just that. Few of us can say we haven't given in to the emotion of Jealousy when someone we love, loves another. Even those fleeting feelings of envy that set upon us when someone acquires the material things over which we swoon have the potential to push us into the enemy's Jealousy snare.

The words of Iago to Othello in Shakespeare's famous

play, *Othello*, ring true: "O, beware, my lord, of Jealousy; It is the green-eyed monster that doth mock the meat it feeds upon..." Those of us on the path to eternity understand that even more than this, Jealousy is an act of the sinful nature; the Apostle Paul includes it in his listing of acts that if practiced will keep believers from inheriting the kingdom of God (Galatians 5:19-21). In his epistle, James writes, *"For where you have envy and selfish ambition, there you will find disorder and every evil practice."* (James 3:16) Paul bluntly asks *"For since there is jealousy and quarreling among you, are you not worldly?"* (1 Corinthians 3:3) A Jealous spirit belongs to the secular world; it cannot reside in the heart of the believer who has committed to following Jesus.

Reflection

What makes you Jealous? Is this a pitfall with which you struggle? What counsel can you offer someone who finds this subject especially challenging?

Day 12

Pride

Pride goes before destruction, a haughty spirit before a fall.
Proverbs 16:18

Just ahead of me two disciples are discussing our last pitfall. One of them speaks of how difficult it was to avoid it. The other declares, "Yes, it was rather a challenge for most of you; but thankfully I'm more alert than most and manage to walk uprightly on the path with little trouble." *Umm*, I thought. *Do I detect a little self-exaltation in that attitude?* As we continue on the road, I sense our next pitfall just might be the subtle snare of Pride.

One of the dictionary's definitions for Pride is "elation arising from some act, possession or relationship, i.e. 'parental Pride.'" It's often this sense of Pride that believers refer to as "holy Pride." The general conclusion being that it's okay to feel elation or Pride when one has excelled, or a loved one has met expectations or achieved desired goals. The feeling of "reasonable or justifiable self-respect" coupled with Pride in others provides the construct for the slippery slope of this pitfall. The questions for believers seeking to avoid the snare are complex. Can a Prideful spirit be holy? What distinguishes elation from Pride? What mask does Pride wear to hide itself from the faithful? We pause, open our guidebook and seek therein guidance for this leg of the journey.

In the Gospel of Luke, Jesus tells the parable of the Pharisee and the Tax Collector. (Luke 18:9-14) As the Bible prefaces, Jesus addressed the story to those who were confident of their own righteousness and looked down on everyone else. Both men were praying in the temple. The Pharisee prayed about himself and how he was better than other men. The Tax Collector said simply, *"God, have mercy on me, a sinner."* Jesus says only the tax collector went home justified before God, and He concluded, *"For everyone who exalts himself will be humbled and he who humbles himself will be exalted."* In the holiest of settings—the temple—there was nothing holy in the Pharisee's Prideful spirit. Quite the opposite; it was the spirit of humility to which Jesus pointed as the better way. As believers, we must be wary of self-praise; of lauding what we do or accomplish as evidence of our greatness; of forgetting that our successes are gifts from God and He alone deserves the praise and the honor. Believers' responses to success are always punctuated with, "To God be the glory."

In his epistle to believers in Rome, Paul advises *"Do not think of yourself more highly than you ought..."* In other words, don't model the example of the disciples James and John before they finally understood the essence of discipleship. You recall their audacious request to Jesus one day. *"Let one of us sit at your right and the other at your left in your glory."* (Mark 10:37) Translated in 21st century speak: "Lord, of all your disciples, we are the two You should appoint to these exalted positions in Your kingdom." I've always wondered what made the disciples ask Jesus to do this. Was it something they had done, or was it just hubris? Perhaps they were like we are at times; feeling we should be rewarded for our efforts to follow Jesus: appointed by the pastor to chair the anniversary committee, or direct the choir, or lead the Bible study class. True believers do not serve and follow the Savior expecting any rewards or recognition for their faith; only the reward of the journey's eventual end matters to them.

Despite its subtlety, Pride's greatest danger is its destructiveness. All too often as our chapter verse reminds us, Pride goes before a fall. King Nebuchadnezzar's Prideful proclamation, *"Is not this the great Babylon I have built as the royal residence, by my mighty power and for the glory of my majesty?"* is a prime biblical example. (Daniel 4:30) As soon as he had spoken those words, God took away all he had and drove him from his kingdom. Why? Because the king forgot "from whom all blessings flow." His fall was sudden and lasted until the time set by God for his restoration. Not until after the chastening caused by his Pride was he able to make a new proclamation, *"Now, I, Nebuchadnezzar, praise and exalt and glorify the King of heaven, because everything he does is right and all his ways are just. And those who walk in pride he is able to humble."* (Daniel 4:37) The message is stark, but clear for us traversing the path to heaven. The secular successes to which we point as evidence of our abilities and by which we define our status in society are hollow if God has not authored the plan for and implementation of them. Unless we build upon His plan for the foundation of our lives, we chance losing what we craft.

Imitating Christ is what believers are called to do. We know that even though He could have exercised His divinity,

He chose not to. As Paul writes in chapter two of Philippians, *"Your attitude should be the same as that of Jesus Christ: who, being in very nature God, did not consider equality with God something to be grasped, but made himself nothing, taking the very nature of a servant, being made in human likeness."* Jesus did not exalt Himself; He allowed God to do the honors. So, too, must we who travel the path to eternity resist the snare of Pride in every facet of our lives; we are not puffed up doughboys. Rather we emulate Jesus by humbling ourselves in service to others to the glory and honor of God.

Reflection

Why is it so easy to point to Prideful attitudes in others and not recognize it in ourselves? Have you ever experienced Pride's destructive power? What precautions can you take to avoid this snare of the Adversary?

Day 13

QUARRELING

He who loves a quarrel loves sin...

Proverbs 17:19

Today's cloudy overcast does more than just hide the sunshine; it seems to be touching spirits as we continue on the path. Is prickliness to be the order of the day? I pray not, as we know that being vexed or irritated can, among other things, lead to the pitfall of Quarreling. That pretty much describes what happened to Abram and Lot as recorded in Genesis 13:5-11 of our guidebook. As the uncle and nephew traveled with their ever-growing flocks of livestock, their herdsmen began to quarrel over land usage. The Bible doesn't record any incidents of violence between the two groups, but contentiousness reached a point where the Quarreling had to be addressed. In verse 8, Abram says to Lot, *"Let us not have any quarreling between you and me, or between your herdsmen and mine, for we are brothers."*

    This early biblical reference to Quarreling as behavior to avoid provides the perspective for dealing with conflict. When conflicts escalate to the point of Quarreling, the spirit of unity Jesus desires in His followers is lost. Now I know at this point you're thinking, "Are you saying we shouldn't express our opinions if they differ from someone else's; that a point expressed against something is sin; that arguing is wrong?" Let me clarify. To argue is to give reasons for or against something; to persuade by giving reasons, usually in discussion. Quarrelling's very nature suggests contentiousness or belligerence; an emotional response to conflict by fault-finding or disputing. Consider Paul's advice to the believers when he writes, *"Don't have anything to do with foolish and stupid arguments, because you know they produce quarrels. And the Lord's servant must not quarrel..."* (2 Timothy 2:23-24)

The apostle goes on to say that when the believer is faced with opposition, it is incumbent upon him to be kind, not resentful, so that he can teach and gently instruct. (2 Timothy 2:24-25) In other words, when conflict arises, Quarreling will not bring about a spirit of unity, which is the goal. A well-spoken argument might, but a quarrelsome response will surely not. The writer of Proverbs is succinct on this point: *Patience calms a quarrel.* (Proverbs 15:18)

If further proof is needed to understand Quarreling as a potential pitfall on this path on which we tread, we need look only at Jesus. If ever anyone had cause for Quarreling, He did. How often was He challenged, disputed, or criticized by His primary opponents, the Pharisees or teachers of the law? In every encounter with the potential to erupt into verbal conflict, the Gospel accounts show the Savior responding without rancor or contentiousness. Giving no cause for dispute, He replied in reasoned measure by quoting the law, interpreting the law, or teaching via a parable.

When some of His contenders confronted Him— *"Why*

do your disciples break the tradition of the elders? They don't wash their hands before they eat!"—Jesus answered, *"And why do you break the command of God for the sake of your tradition?"* They wanted to engage in sophomoric debate to snare Him, but He deflected their efforts by interpreting one of God's commandments. A moment of conflict that could have escalated into raucous Quarreling was averted. If the One whose name we claim resisted the snare of Quarreling, can we do any less? Let us remember: we are in the world but we are not of the world. Quarreling is a worldly behavior we do not emulate.

Reflection

Are you easily drawn into Quarreling? Are you renowned for your "tit-for-tat" repartee? When your efforts to argue your position or opinion with reason and calmness are shot down, do you pause to regroup or immediately step up to the quarreler's plate? If this behavior of Quarreling is your challenge, what measures can you take to lessen its snare?

Day 14

Guilt

God made him who had no sin to be sin for us, so that in him we might become the righteousness of God.
                                    2 Corinthians 5:21

As the journey continues, I've noticed that some of my fellow travelers are falling by the wayside. More often than not they are the ones who have either been snared for a while in a pitfall or tethered closely on the brink of one. An aura of failure hoovers above them. I suspect the Adversary is playing upon this sense of self-reproach to pull them into the mire of the pitfall up ahead: Guilt.

As believers, we accept that Jesus died for our sins to return us to right relationship with God. And because of His sacrifice on that cross, we are forgiven of our sins; we need not carry the burden of Guilt that can weigh us down. Yet this cerebral understanding doesn't make its way to the heart and spirit of some saints; they struggle still with Guilt, making them prime targets for the enemy. These travelers carry feelings of culpability for offenses they've committed and find themselves responding as did some of our biblical ancestors when they were Guilt-ridden; with strategies of excuse, denial, suppression. Consider Adam's and Eve's responses when confronted directly by God for their disobedience as recorded in Genesis, chapter three.

God asked, *"Have you eaten from the tree that I commanded you not to eat from?"* Adam: *"The woman you put here with me—she gave me some fruit from the tree, and I ate it."* Eve: *"The serpent deceived me, and I ate."* Notice that neither the man nor the woman owned their actions, or asked for forgiveness. Excuses for disobedience give rise to feelings of Guilt, and sprout lasting consequences. In the case of Adam and Eve, they produced the seminal estrangement of humankind from God.

Even God's servant-king, David, knew the snare of Guilt when he sought to suppress his sinful actions with subterfuge by ordering the husband of the woman with whom he had committed adultery to sleep with her to cover the pregnancy resulting from the sin. When that scheme failed, he ordered his commander to place the husband in a position in the battle that would ensure his death. (2 Samuel: 11-12) Suppression of truth creates Guilt; and even when sin is confessed, there are consequences with which one must deal. How are we to understand the Guilt felt by the disciple Peter when he denied knowing Jesus in the courtyard three times, just as Jesus had foretold he would. Scripture says, *"And he went outside and wept bitterly."* (Luke 22:54-62) Denial of truth inevitably produces Guilt; and that Guilt can be heart-wrenching.

The psalmist poses the question, *"If you, O Lord, kept a record of sins, O Lord who could stand? But with you there is forgiveness..."* (Psalm 130:3-4) Ah, here then is our hope! Jesus Christ fulfilled the scripture and rescued us from sin and Guilt with His death and resurrection. His sacrificial act justified us with the Father. (1 Corinthians 6:11) As Paul writes in Romans 8:1, *"There is therefore now no condemnation for those who are in Christ Jesus."* Guilt can be laid aside if we follow the teachings of 1 John 1:9, *"If we confess our sins, he is faithful and just to forgive us our sins and to cleanse us from all unrighteousness."* These words of assurance from our guidebook give us the power to resist the pull of a Guilty conscience. Yes, we've all failed at some point to live up to the call of Jesus; we have erred and gone astray. Yet, believers must not allow the weight of Guilt for past or present failings to pull them off the path and into the pit. Instead, those walking this path to eternity heed the words of the writer of Hebrews when he encourages us to *"…draw near to God with a sincere heart in full assurance of faith, having our hearts sprinkled to cleanse us from a guilty conscience."* (Hebrews 10:22-23)

Reflection

Guilty feelings are common to the human experience. At one time or another, we feel Guilt for ill-spoken words, for vengeful actions, for schemes and dreams that are outside God's will, for thoughts we know are ungodly. How do we turn Guilt around? What do we do to avoid it in the first place? Does unresolved Guilt impede your walk with the Lord? What will you do about it?

Day 15

DESIRES

What the righteous desire will be granted.
Proverbs 10:24b

There's something to be said for R and R—Rest and Reflection—on this journey. When we make time for both, we are able to draw from the well of our guidebook just what we need. Just ask our fellow travelers who seemed ready to throw in the towel because of guilt's tentacles. Replenished now with God's energy bar—His Word—they continue the course. Refreshed and desiring the goodness of the Lord to lead them, they rejoin us on the path. Our thoughts, and soon our conversations, turn to what we as believers understand might be the next pitfall: our Desires.

Desires—cravings, longings—seem imprinted in the human DNA. From the earliest years of desiring parental love and approval to the escalating Desires as we grow for things that give pleasure and satisfaction, the human capacity for desiring has few boundaries.

The dictionary defines desire as a "conscious impulse toward something that promises enjoyment or satisfaction in its attainment." And therein rests the potential for Desires to lead believers astray. Knowing what Desires are pleasing to God and avoiding those that are not is the only way believers can avoid this snare. We've been on the path long enough now to know what to do next: check our guidebook.

The day's scripture reference gives us the cornerstone for discernment regarding Desires. It is reinforced by Proverbs 11:6, that teaches *"...but the unfaithful are trapped by evil desires."* Some things we desire are not necessarily evil in and of themselves. But when Desires take us beyond the quality of life basics—health, provisions, work—we risk crossing the line into enemy territory, i.e. societal trappings, and being caught by one of the most common unrighteous Desires: coveting: desiring to have what others have. The tenth commandment sets the requirement for the believer regarding this kind of desire. It says, *"You shall not set your desire on..."* anything belonging to others. When we covet what others have, we fall into this pitfall.

Taking the theme of negative Desires even further, the Apostle Paul doesn't mince words when he writes, *"People who want to get rich fall into temptation and a trap and into many foolish and harmful desires that plunge men into ruin and destruction."* (1 Timothy 6:9) Other admonitions against unrighteous Desires pepper our guidebook. Romans 13:14 advises, *"...and do not think about how to gratify the desires of the sinful nature."* Why? Galatians 5:16-17 answers. *"So, I say, live by the Spirit, and you will not gratify the desires of the sinful nature. For the sinful nature desires what is contrary to the Spirit and the Spirit what is contrary to the sinful nature."* The Apostle Peter pleads, *"Dear friends, I urge you... to abstain from sinful desires, which war against your soul."* (1 Peter 2:11)

Our understandings sharpen as we delve more into the

guidebook. We ask ourselves which of our cravings or longings or impulses toward things that promise us satisfaction if we attain them are within God's design for His followers. We read in Psalm 37:4, *"Delight yourself in the Lord and he will give you the desires of your heart."* Really? The promotion; the big house; the new car; the dream vacation; the prestigious college; the stock portfolio; the successful career; the gorgeous wife; the rich husband; the brilliant kid—all this He'll give me, and all I must do is delight in Him? As excitement grows among the travelers, someone asks, "What do you think the Lord means by delighting ourselves in Him? I mean, how do we do that?" This sobriety of thought settles our whimsical fantasies and we give attention again to the resource. To delight in the Lord, we conclude, means we find our satisfaction in Him and in what He considers worthy of possessing or attaining. In Hosea 6:6, God says He Desires mercy, extending to others that which He has shown us. The Apostle Paul teaches we are to desire the greater gifts of faith, hope, and love. (1Corinthians 12:31) And he goes on to declare that spiritual gifts are what we should desire. (1Corinthians 14:1)

We conclude as the path leads us onward, that the Desires that meet God's gold standard are ones that move us outside our own cravings and into the realm of the other. Yes, we want Him to bless us with whatever will enable us to live for Him. But along with that, we desire to attain the very attributes of His Spirit. For if we are imbued with His Spirit, if it lives in us, our first and default longings will not mimic those of the world. Instead we will desire that which blesses others through our attainment of it. And it will be in that righteousness that God grants us our Desires.

Reflection

Looking back over your life, what have been your most fervent Desires? Did what you desired change over the seasons of your life? How so? Today, what are your Desires? Do you think they please God? Is this pitfall a challenge for you? Why or why not?

Day 16

SPEAKER'S REMORSE

He who holds his tongue is wise.

Proverbs 10:19

We've come to understand that though the destination for all believers is the same, we travel the path to reach it in ways uniquely ours. This insight explains why some of us proceed with a steady clip, some trudge along, bringing up the rear and others sprint ahead, seeming to glide over pitfalls as if they're not even there. We hear the latter group shout back at us, "Watch out for Speaker's Remorse. It's the pitfall just ahead of you." Oh my, we know what they mean. For who among us has not suffered from the condition of yielding control to the appendage in our mouth we call a tongue.

The psalmist gives sound counsel when he writes, *"I will watch my ways and keep my mouth from sin."* (Psalm 39:1) Perhaps the most graphic illustration of the danger of this pitfall is painted by the apostle James as he offers real life examples of how deadly the tongue can be; how untamable. The tongue he declares is like a spark that ignites a forest fire; though small, it *"… is a fire, a world of evil among the parts of the body. It corrupts the whole person, sets the whole course of his life on fire, and is itself set on fire by hell."* (James 3:5-6) Continuing his denunciation, the apostle declares that though man has been able to tame all kinds of animals that inhabit the earth, he has not done the same with the tongue: *"...but no man can tame the tongue. It is a restless evil, full of deadly poison."* (James 3:7-8)

As we read these scriptures, few of us plead innocence. Ill-spoken words have indeed flowed from our mouths. We've felt the chagrin of having spoken without thinking. We recall the times when with our tongue we provoked or hurt others. We swore (sometimes, like the proverbial sailor); we shouted hurtful words; we let fly the unkindest verbal arrows we could aim. Unfortunately, too many of us marginalize our faith with the rationalization that if we don't fire back verbally, we are weak; that standing our ground with our tongue in battle mode is the preferred posture. In that stance we empower the tongue to give tit-for-tat; to strike first; to wound. We do all this while at the same time professing our faith as believers. We exemplify James' words: *"With the tongue we praise our Lord and Father, and with it we curse men, who have been made in God's likeness. Out of the same mouth come praise and cursing."* (James 3:9-10) It's important to note too that the tongue's ability to utter obscenities is not its only hazard. Some folk never speak a curse word their entire lives; I can honestly say my mother never did. But that didn't mean her tongue was above reproach. When we were both young, there were times that her stinging words of rebuke were so painful, I would have preferred a *#@! word! It is true that *"reckless words pierce like a sword."* (Proverbs 12:18)

As we seek ways to avoid this snare, it is helpful to

remember that cursing and hurtful words are not the only danger of the tongue. It also is the mechanism that exposes what resides in the heart; and what resides in the heart defines the measure of the man or woman. Jesus declares, *"For out of the overflow of the heart the mouth speaks."* (Matthew 12:34) The Apostle Paul advises the faithful to avoid all acts of the sinful nature; and that includes sin that lurks in the heart and is expressed with the tongue. (Galatians 5:16-21) The believer must strive to speak words that bring healing; words that speak wisdom; words that speak truth; words that speak love. Jesus gives a sobering rationale for why we so endeavor when He says, *"But I tell you that men will have to give account on the Day of Judgment for every careless word they have spoken. For by your words you will be acquitted, and by your words you will be condemned."* (Matthew 12:36-37) Finally, the believer also understands that the heart which is the repository for what spills from the mouth must be free of anything not of God; and this is only possible when God's Spirit abides therein. For where the Spirit of the Lord is, so is He. Such hearts when so filled will harbor nothing that might precipitate a tumble into the pitfall of Speaker's Remorse.

Reflection

Is this pitfall one of your challenge points? Do you often suffer Speaker's Remorse? What faith sustaining strategies do you employ to avoid tyranny of the tongue?

Day 17

Judgment

Therefore let us stop passing judgment on one another.
Romans 14:13

As the path stretches ahead beyond our ability to see its direction, we continue the journey. So many of us came close to slipping into the last pitfall that we've agreed to hold each other accountable for the words we speak. We are unaware that the enemy gleefully applauds this decision. His next pitfall—Judgment—is perfectly positioned.

Perhaps one of the more familiar stories of Judgment in the New Testament is the account recorded in chapter eight of the Gospel of John. As Jesus is teaching in the temple courts, He is confronted by the experts of the law and the Pharisees, who have with them a woman they allege was caught in the act of adultery. (We are left to wonder the whereabouts of the man who was involved but…) Citing the Law of Moses, the accusers contend the woman must be stoned; and ask Jesus, *"Now what do you say?"* His immediate and strange response has ignited theological discourse ever since. Silently, he bends down and begins to write on the ground with His finger. What in the world could He have been writing: perhaps scriptures, or the names of the accusers and their sins? As He writes, they continue to bombard Him with queries until finally Jesus lifts His head and says to them, *"If any one of you is without sin, let him be the first to throw a stone at her."* As Jesus returns to writing on the ground, the silence is numbing. One by one the woman's accusers steal away. Jesus straightens up and asks, *"Woman, where are they? Has no one condemned you?" "No,"* she replies. *"Then neither do I condemn you,"* Jesus declares. And He tells her to go and leave her life of sin.

Obviously, the woman's accusers weren't in the crowd that day when Jesus launched His ministry from a mountainside and delivered His Sermon on the Mount as recorded in the fifth through seventh chapters of the Gospel of Matthew. He taught them the tenets they must embrace if they are to live a life of faith. His admonitions regarding the pitfall of Judgment ring down through the millennia to us today: *"Do not judge; or you too will be judged. For in the same way you judge others, you will be judged, and with the measure you use, it will be measured to you."* (Matthew 7:1-2)

The Apostle James asks succinctly, *"who are you to judge your neighbor?"* (James 4:12) This simple question is a lightning strike for many of us. With a measure of consternation and often varying degrees of guilt, we remember how quickly we are prone to judge others. As a retired secondary school English teacher, I still cringe whenever I hear someone misspeak Standard English. I have to stop myself from voicing or thinking the inevitable negative Judgments that follow if I don't. Many a believer struggles to avoid even casual Judgments: *She doesn't have the body to wear that dress! As big as he is, the last thing he needs to buy is some candy. Those people holding up those "I'm hungry" signs just want money to buy...* It doesn't matter whether we voice these thoughts or think them to ourselves; they reveal our propensity for judging others. We forget that Galatian 2:6 says, "*God does not judge by external appearance.*" If God doesn't, why would we? In those instances when the discretions and flaws and yes, *sins*, of others become public knowledge do we have license then to judge? Notice that Jesus in no way disputed the charges of adultery; and the woman made no claim of innocence. Jesus challenged the hypocrisy of the accusers who felt they could point to the woman's sin as if they had none of their own. More than anyone else He could have judged; but He did not. Instead He chose to bestow mercy and a second chance.

It is so easy to find fault and accuse others; to judge by appearance, to judge in ignorance, to judge with hubris. Even when someone's sin is horrendous and vile and senseless and is arbitrated within our legal systems, believers cannot forget that sin is sin; that no sin trumps another, or as Paul writes, "*...for all have sinned and fall short of the glory of God.*" (Romans 3:23) As believers we have our opinions, but we do not think of ourselves as less flawed than the other guy. Rather we keep in mind the wisdom of Oswald Chambers' words: "Every wrong thing that I see in you, God locates in me... I have never met the man I could despair of after discerning what lies in me apart from the grace of God." (*My Utmost for His Highest*)

Reflection

How quick are you to judge others? On what are those Judgments usually based? Do you think all sins are equal, or do you rate some as more offensive than others?

Day 18

LYING

Whoever of you desires to see many good days, keep your tongue from evil and your lips from speaking lies.

Psalm 34:13

As we set forth today, we're a little skittish. That last pitfall around which we teetered was difficult. More and more on this path we have chosen to follow, our understanding of what total commitment to the Savior means has deepened. Things we thought inconsequential before assume greater significance. The next pitfall serves as a prime example.

We all recall Aesop's fable read to pre-school age children by parents or teachers entitled, "The Boy Who Cried Wolf." It is a tale of the downside of not telling the truth. Twice a shepherd boy cries out, "Wolf! Wolf! The wolf is chasing the sheep!" Each time when the villagers respond and discover there is no wolf, they warn the errant boy to save his warning for when the threat is real. Finally, a wolf does appear; but when the boy cries out for help no one comes. Later when the little fellow did not return to the village, the townspeople go up the hill to investigate. There they discover the boy weeping. The wolf had scattered the sheep and he was distraught because no one came to help when he sounded the alarm.

An old man of the village spoke the moral of the story: "Nobody believes a liar… even when he is telling the truth."

Long before Aesop penned this fable, we recall the story of the first lie ever told, by none other than the father of lies, the enemy of our faith. He asked the woman if God had said she must not eat from any tree in the garden. She responded that was true; if she ate fruit from the tree in the middle of the garden, she would die. And the enemy in the guise of a serpent spoke the seminal lie: *"You will surely not die."* (Genesis 3:1-4) And thus was laid the foundation for the human proclivity for Lying.

God knew this tendency to lie would be an issue for His people. He addressed it in the various laws He gave to them: "Do not lie. Do not deceive one another." (Leviticus 19:11) These stark words of guidance resonate today; or they should. The reality of these post-biblical times is that Lying is somehow not that big a deal anymore. We've even invented the term "white lie" to describe lies termed harmless or trivial, especially if told to avoid hurting someone's feelings. In a world and culture that has co-opted the story of Jesus' birth; the white lie of Santa Claus is as ingrained as baby Jesus in the manger. Even believers incorporate both in their celebrations; though often with a tinge of guilt. The writer of Proverbs pulls no punches when he writes, *"The Lord detests lying lips, but he delights in men who are truthful."* (Proverbs 12:22)

It is a struggle; either we lie or we tell the truth. Does it apply to every word we speak? Are we only guilty if we spread false rumors, slander, and gossip, or exaggerate? Are we free of this sin if we do not speak malicious lies that harm or deceive? Does our hypocrisy count against us? Are we Lying when we distort perceptions? If we accept the dictionary definitions of what it means to lie, then these actions condemn us. Consider the story of Ananias and his wife Sapphira, as told in Acts 5:3-9. Though converts to the faith, they allowed self-interest to distort their judgment. When the Apostle Peter questioned them regarding their actions, they lied; and subsequently died as a direct result. The Apostle Paul teaches, *"Do not lie to each other, since you have taken off your old self with its practices, and have put on the new self..."* (Colossians 3":9-10)

The danger of this pitfall is its slippery slope. Lying has become such the norm, we accept its shady coverings of innuendo, half-truths, unsubstantiated accusations, and misstated facts, and because most of us are not perpetrators of the big lies that bombard us on television or in newsprint, we shrug off the little lies that permeate our everyday coming and going. Unlike the politician in the news, we didn't lie about the polluted water that plagued our city; but we did make that slanderous remark about the neighbor across the street. Can Lying be rated in egregiousness from one to ten? Perhaps we avoid slipping into this pitfall by once again heeding the words found in our guidebook: *"There are six things the Lord hates, seven that are detestable to him: ...a lying tongue...a false witness who pours out lies..."* (Proverbs 6:16-19) As the faithful on this path to eternity, we accept we must never exchange God's truth as revealed in His word for lies.

Reflection

Lying is so easy, we sometimes are not conscious of it. Do

you tell the "Little Lies?" "Yes, Santa is real." "Um, that looks ok on you." "No, I'm fine. I don't need any help." "I don't know who ate the last piece of cake." What about in your professional life? Are you expected to lie for the common good or to advance the goals of the company or institution? Do your actions ever betray your words? Is that Lying? How much of a challenge is this pitfall for you?

Day 19

SINFULNESS

For there is no one who does not sin.

1 Kings 8:46

For reasons yet unknown we sense consternation among the faith-walkers. Maybe it's the pace at which we are moving; it seems to have slowed, as if we are bogged down by something. Skirting around the path's perimeter, an intrepid believer shouts, "My goodness! No wonder we're moving at a snail's pace. The pitfall ahead is large enough to swallow us all; it's the snare of Sinfulness."

The fluttering of consternation is an apt response. Each believer knows this pitfall has the potential to derail anyone on the journey; and for obvious reasons. The human tendency to sin is a spiritual plague for which there is no cure; and though Jesus died on the cross as expiation for our sins, we still fall short and give life to the words noted in the day's scripture. Sinfulness casts such a wide net the believer is hard-pressed to avoid it. Its tentacles easily entangle and there are few if any places where it is not present.

As always, our go-to guide for dealing with all we encounter is our guidebook. Therein we discover what "thus says the

Lord." John defines sin when he writes, *"in fact, sin is lawlessness."* (I John 3:4) This lawlessness, or transgression of God's will, can occur in thought, (I John 3:15) word, (Matthew 5:22) or deed. (Romans 1:32) Phrased simply, sin is rebellion against God. Glancing backward to our biblical history, we know that sin entered the world through a disobedient act. That deed which transgressed God's will spread like an epidemic through succeeding generations. But because we serve a long-suffering God, He didn't completely give up on His creation. In a culminating effort to save us from the consequences of our waywardness, He sent His Son on a specific mission to deliver us. Jesus' sacrifice and promise of eternity with Him are why we traverse the path we're on. That path would be uncomplicated, excepting one thing: sin. Yes, sin is a conundrum for the faith-walker; we accept the gift of our salvation from sin while continuing to commit the sins from which we've been saved. How and/or why is that possible?

The guidebook reminds us, *"all have sinned and fall short of the glory of God."* (Romans 3:23) Though we understand that *"No one who lives in him keeps on sinning,"* (1 John 3:6) we nonetheless struggle to live righteously. Our very nature as human beings predisposes us to sinful behavior which is contrary to the will of God. The scriptures tell us exactly what comprises a sinful nature; the acts of which are clearly enunciated in Galatians 5:19-21. Yet even as intellectually we get it, our experiences as believers mimic those of the Apostle Paul. Who among us cannot claim his words as our own: *"I do not understand what I do. For what I want to do I do not do, but what I hate, I do… For what I do is not the good I want to do; no, the evil I do not want to do—this I keep on* *doing." (*Romans 7:14-19) By our actions we show ourselves slaves to sin; and seemingly forget that the *"wages of sin is death."* (Romans 6:23)

Such a pitfall seems almost impossible to avoid; yet we have as stepping stones over and around it the amazing grace and mercy of God. For it is by His grace through Jesus Christ our Lord that we are more than conquerors. His mercy is sufficient to forgive us our missteps and free us from whatever seeks to entangle. Sin may be ever present, a constant threat seeking to bar the path. Thankfully, we serve a God who, like the Eveready Bunny, never stops running. He is a tireless supplier of the power, wisdom, and guidance believers need to avoid the pitfall and stay on the path.

Reflection

Do you consider yourself a sinner, even though you've accepted Jesus as Lord of your life? To what kinds of sin are you most prone: thought, word, or deed? Is your faith-walk anything like Paul's? What spiritual disciplines help you stay afloat in the sea of Sinfulness common to the human experience?

Day 20

SORROW

There is a time for everything ... a time to weep... a time to mourn...

Ecclesiastes 3:1-4

Ever determined, we step carefully on the path after that last pitfall. The enormity of its destructive potential casts a gloom, marking us easier targets for the snare ahead: Sorrow and its many cousins—sadness, despondency, desolation, heartache, grief, and woe.

As believers, we are familiar with our guidebook's theological teaching, commonly known as "A Time for Everything" in chapter 3, verses 1-8 of Ecclesiastes. These words speak to the human experience; its shifts and twists, fickleness and uncertainty, changes and vicissitudes. As surely as we live, at some point on this journey home to the Father we will face circumstances that give life to Sorrow and/or its relatives.

The dictionary defines Sorrow as "a feeling of deep distress caused by loss, disappointment, or other misfortune suffered by oneself or others." We see it most poignantly in the biblical account of Hannah, one of two wives (during a time when such was the cultural norm) of Elkanah. Hannah's inability to have children, as did the second wife, caused her great distress. Year after year the fickleness of fertility reduced her to tears and despondency, and the provocations of her counterpart because of her barrenness further aggravated her situation. Though she was a woman of faith who worshipped God and kept the laws of her time, she was not spared Sorrow's arrow. When accused of drunkenness by the priest as she prayed, she spoke to that Sorrow, *"Not so, my Lord. I am a woman who is deeply troubled... I have been praying here out of my great anguish and grief."* (1 Samuel 15-16)

It is clear as we keep to the path God has prepared that none of us has come this far without the experiences of loss, disappointment, or misfortune. Sorrow's shapes come in many forms—the heavy heart filled with grief at the loss of loved ones; the downcast countenance of relationship disappointments; the slumping shoulders of career failures; the eyes that mirror physical disabilities. The psalmist's words ring all too true; *"My soul is weary with sorrow."* (Psalm 119:28)

Though the pitfall of Sorrow may seem difficult to avoid, it has only the power to entrap that believers allow it. If we do falter, God has equipped us to escape any lasting hold. We have His counsel in our guidebook. Following His counsel, we can triumph over Sorrow. Though it may linger for a moment as a reaction to life's uncertainties, it does not have the power to prevail.

As the writer of Ecclesiastes teaches, everything has its time: *a time to weep and a time to laugh, a time to mourn and a time to dance.* The psalmist asserts *"weeping may remain for a night, but rejoicing comes in the morning."* (Psalm 30:5) God has promised that His people will "Sorrow no more." With the joy of these words ringing in our hearts, we can bypass this snare and continue the journey.

Reflection

When has Sorrow snared you? How long did you linger in its power? What helped you escape? Is it easier now for you to avoid it, or are you still easy prey? What life circumstances are more apt to send you into its clutches? What can you do differently that might shorten your stay?

Day 21

WORLDLINESS

Do not love the world or anything in the world. If anyone loves the world, the love of the Father is not in him. For everything in the world—the cravings of sinful man, the lust of his eyes and the boasting of what he has and does—comes not from the Father but from the world.

1 John 2:15-16

The cadre of believers with whom we've been in step for some reason seems to be getting smaller. The path doesn't feel as crowded as when we began. Taking closer note of our surroundings, we wonder if perhaps the world's attractions bordering the path are proving more and more irresistible. With that thought the lightbulb comes on; our next pitfall is none other than Worldliness.

The dictionary gives two definitions of the word, Worldliness: "the quality of being experienced and sophisticated" and "concern with material values or ordinary life rather than a spiritual existence." Our guidebook primarily offers insight regarding the second definition. Therein do we come to understand that on this path to eternity, our concerns cannot mirror those of the secular world. The account of

Adam and Eve in Genesis 3:1-7 is our biblical introduction to the human proclivity toward Worldliness. *"When the woman saw that the fruit of the tree was good for food and pleasing to the eye, and also desirable for gaining wisdom, she took some and ate it. She also gave some to her husband, who was with her, and he ate it."* The idea that the knowledge of worldly affairs was so easily within reach was difficult to resist. Who, after all, isn't tempted by the perks of the temporal? Like our nascent ancestors drawn in that moment to what held the promise of being good, had the potential to give pleasure, and gave the assurance of knowledge, we seek and are drawn to these same temptations.

In this self-proclaimed Christian nation, the attainment of the good life is etched in our consciousness from birth as the major pursuit of living. The more education we acquire, the more intelligence we proclaim. The more money we earn, the more we expend on things we deem pleasing and good for our well-being. The key components of our value system are acquisition, self-interest, self-aggrandizement, and favorable appearances masked to hide all deficiencies. And as did those emergent ancestors who tried to hide their nakedness with leaves, we shield ourselves with shallow sophistication in hope of hiding our disobedience from the Creator. The lesson offered us by the writer of Ecclesiastes (2:1-11) regarding the meaninglessness of ambition and acquisition sails by like leaves stirred by a blowing wind. We read and then forget the words of the Apostle Paul in 1 Corintians 3:19: *"For the wisdom of the world is foolishness in God's sight."*

As believers seeking to stay the course on the path we know leads to eternity, we must internalize the teachings in our guidebook, so they anchor us in our faith. We must ignore the adversary's shrewd schemes by remembering John's words: *"The world hates followers of Jesus."* (John 15:19) We must embrace the words of Paul when he reminds us that *"though we live in the world, we do not wage war as the world does."* (2 Corinthians 10:3) And we must clearly hear Titus speak to us that, *"God's grace teaches us to say "No" to ungodliness and worldly passion."* (Titus 2:12)

Finally, James admonishes the faithful to recall that religion acceptable as pure and faultless, is religion that keeps us from being polluted by the world. For friendship with the world is hatred toward God; a friend of the world is an enemy of God. (James 1:26-27; 4:4-10) Yes, the world has its lures and attractions and practices that on the surface seem harmless. That was the adversary's pitch to our fledging ancestors—*"You will not surely die," the serpent said to the woman. "God knows when you eat of it your eyes will be opened, and you will be like God." (Genesis 3:4-5)* We have the lesson of the consequences of their actions to guide us today. The pitfall lines the path, but with due diligence and reliance upon our guidebook we can avoid it.

Reflection

Do you struggle with this pitfall? Is it hard for you to be in the world, but not of the world in your values and actions? What have been your hardest challenges in this area? What helps you refocus your footsteps when you find yourself straying from the path?

Day 22

UNFORGIVENESS

Then Peter came to Jesus and asked, "Lord, how many times shall I forgive my brother when he sins against me? Up to seven times?" Jesus answered, "I tell you, not seven times, but seventy times seven."
                                    Matthew 18:21-22

Though some of our group fell prey to that last pitfall, most managed to stay the course; primarily those who kept their eyes focused on God's word could step over or around it. Scripture instructs that His word is the lamp that lights our path. (Psalm 119:105) Those who ignore that teaching are prone to stumble, as the travelers teetering near the pitfall ahead appear to be doing. Unforgiveness has cast its net.

Society doesn't encourage a spirit of forgiveness as our guidebook prescribes, even though the very nature of God is one of forgiveness. The book of Nehemiah reminds us of this when he writes of our heavenly Father, *"But you are a forgiving God, gracious and compassionate, slow to anger and abounding love."* (Nehemiah (9:17) We need only recall the first demonstration of that forgiving nature when He confronted Adam and Eve with their disobedience, yet spared their lives and gave them another chance; outside the garden, yes, but another chance nonetheless. Well within His power was the execution of the death penalty He had proclaimed if they disobeyed. But almost as a precursor to Jesus' teachings yet to come, God the Father, forgave.

The snare of the spirit of Unforgiveness can easily entrap. Because sin is so rampart and so interwoven in the fabric of our lives, Unforgiveness is often embraced as a normal response when someone is wronged. How often have we heard loved ones of victims of crime or non-intentional destructive acts proclaim their inability to forgive those who are responsible? A typical response is, "I can never forgive him/her/them for the pain caused by what was done." Such a spirit, over time, inevitably leads to bitterness and its potential harms. Then there are those who are unable to forgive themselves for wrongs they've committed, either to themselves or others. They wallow in self-recrimination and refuse the mercy and grace our heavenly Father offers.

Yielding to a spirit of Unforgiveness is an affront to God. If the One who created us is forgiving of our faults and sins, how can we be otherwise? Yes, we may have suffered enormous harm at the hands of others; we may have caused harm to ourselves or others; we may suffer daily the "slings and arrows of outrageous fortune." A forgiving spirit requires we do not "take arms against a sea of troubles…" (Shakespeare's "Hamlet") Scripture abounds with stories that show us a better way. Consider the twins, Jacob and Esau, born to Isaac and Rebekah. In an artful scheme of deception, Jacob tricked his brother out of his rightful inheritance. Yet years later, Esau showed mercy and love in his forgiving spirit when he embraced Jacob after their long separation. (Genesis 25,

27, 32-33) And who doesn't recall one of the more famous stories of forgiveness when one has been wronged as recorded in Genesis 37-50. Joseph, the 11th son of Jacob, was thrown into a pit by his brothers and eventually sold by them into slavery. Such familial tragedy is hard to conceive. Yet, years later when those very brothers came face to face with the brother they thought was dead, and realized he held the power of life or death over them and their families, they were astonished by his reactions. Rather than serve up the justice they deserved for their past crimes, he forgave, embraced, and comforted them. His words stand today as the standard for a forgiving spirit: *"But Joseph said to them, don't be afraid. Am I in the place of God? You intended to harm me, but God intended it for good to accomplish what is now being done, the saving of many lives... And he reassured them and spoke kindly to them."* (Genesis 50:19-21)

Finally, can we forget the saga of the woman caught in adultery? Can we see Jesus bent over, writing in the dirt as her accusers demand that she be punished by stoning? As their demands grew more strident, scripture reports Jesus straightened up and said to them, *"If anyone of you is without sin, let him be the first to throw a stone at her."* (John 8:1-2) As we know, not one stone was thrown. Instead, Jesus offered her mercy and grace, and gave her permission to forgive herself by turning away from the sin of which she was guilty. Always the temptation toward Unforgiveness will shadow our steps on the path to eternity. But we who claim Jesus must remember the wisdom of our guidebook: *"Forgive as the Lord forgave you."* (Colossians 3:13); *"Be kind and compassionate to one another, forgiving each other, just as in Christ God forgave you."* (Ephesians 4:32)

Reflection

When you think of your attitude toward others who have wronged you in some form or fashion, describe your feelings. Are you a grudge-holder? What is your first reaction when someone does something painfully wrong to you or your loved ones? Is this sense of being a forgiving person no matter the circumstances difficult for you to embrace?

Day 23

UNCERTAINTY

Let us hold unswervingly to the hope we profess, for he who promised is faithful.

Hebrews 10:23

Someone is singing as we continue the journey today. The haunting words of that old gospel hymn, "*Walk with me, Lord,*" fill the air. A voice reminiscent of the great gospel songstress, Mahalia Jackson serenades us and we walk in rhythm with it. Indeed, as the path stretches ahead and we encounter the enemy's unending attempts to dissuade us from staying the course, we know the truth of these lyrics. They remind us that we need Jesus to walk with us on the journey and the truth of that counsel resonates as we see ahead our next pitfall—Uncertainty, which is a first cousin of *Doubt*, who we met earlier.

The writer of Hebrews urges believers to cast aside any Uncertainty in living the faith of Jesus Christ. Once we proclaim Him Lord and Savior and place our hope in what He teaches and commands, we cannot be wishy-washy, i.e. weak or ineffectual in living what we profess. Indeed, if in that profession of faith we truly believe God is faithful to whatever He promises, we can imitate the patriarch, Abraham. Promised by God that his offspring would one day equal the number of stars in heaven, he did not hesitate to carry out God's command to kill the son through whom that promise was to bear fruit. It would have been so easy at this juncture for him to waver, to question, to give Uncertainty a foothold. But he did not. Instead Abraham cast Uncertainty aside and moved forward in faith that a God omnipotent enough to make such an outlandish proclamation in the first place was surely able to bring it to fruition. How? Abraham didn't know; the command to sacrifice Isaac seemed to refute the promise. What Abraham did know was this was the same God who had faithfully orchestrated his life since the day the Lord said to him, *"Leave your country, your people and your father's household and go to the land I will show you. I will make you into a great nation and I will bless you."* (Genesis 12:1-2) There is no rationale for Uncertainty with a God who assures us with these words recorded by the prophet Isaiah: *"...so is my word that goes out from my mouth: It will not return to me empty, but will accomplish what I desire and achieve the purpose for which I sent it."* (Isaiah 55:11)

The dictionary gives as a synonym for Uncertainty—dubiety; it means wavering between conclusions. That is the snare someone plagued by Uncertainty in their faith faces. Having reached the conclusion that Jesus is the answer, the key to salvation and eternal life, believers on the edge of slipping into this pitfall go back and forth in their trust of God's assurances. They waver in the face of life's trials and temptations; they are the double-minded folk James speaks of when he writes, *"But when he asks, he must believe and not doubt, because he who doubts is like a wave of the sea, blown and tossed by the wind… he is a double-minded man, unstable in all he does."* (James 1:6-8) On this path we have chosen, we must be alert always to anything that might cause us to live aimlessly and without clear purpose. This first cousin of *Doubt* is one such thing with the potential to stall our walk of faith.

The singing continues as we walk; the words seeming to stir around us. Yes, with Jesus alongside, we can sidestep Uncertainty; and continue our journey in faith to the promised land.

Reflection

Are your more likely to feel uncertain of God's promises when your circumstances are difficult? If you had to rate the issues you confront regularly, what would rank first as the one that creates the most Uncertainty? In your opinion, is there a difference between doubtfulness and Uncertainty? Why or why not?

Day 24

Weakness

The spirit is willing, but the body is weak.

Matthew 26:41

Always energized after we've avoided the adversary's snare, we begin the new day determined to stay on course. Spirits are high as we walk together toward glory. Then, with no warning, the path meanders and we lose sight of some of the believers ahead. We've been on the road long enough now to know what this might mean—another pitfall has opened and the faithful ahead are fighting to avoid it. As they struggle, we are reminded of the disciples left to watch and pray in the Garden of Gethsemane. The willingness of their spirit was overcome by the Weakness of their bodies and they succumbed. Such is the case with those now falling prey to the next pitfall: Weakness.

As Jesus prepared to pray in solitude at one of the darkest moments of His ministry, He took Peter, James, and John with Him and said to them, *"Keep watch with me."* (Matthew 26:38) When He returned sometime later, He found them asleep. Chiding them, He said, *"Watch and pray so that you will not fall into temptation. The spirit is willing, but the body is weak."* (Matthew 26:40-41) Succumbing to temptation is a frailty of the human experience. It reveals Weakness as a snare forever nipping at our heals. What caused Eve and Adam to eat the forbidden fruit? What made King David bed Uriah's wife? What seduced Judas into betrayal? What prompted Peter to deny Christ? In every instance of disobedience or failure, it was the betrayal of mind and body that caused our biblical ancestors to give in to Weakness.

We are no different. Our tongue speaks when it should be quiet and remains silent when it should speak. Our body moves when it should stand still and stands still when it should spring into action. Our mind wanders from the truth when it should remain focused and steadfast. Our eyes lust for what postures as pleasant and desirable rather than seeking to see with discernment and wisdom. In moments of crisis, we tremble in fear rather than standing in faith upon the word of God. In short, we give free rein to Weakness in body, mind, and spirit to wreak havoc; to push us off the path we trod.

The dictionary provides several definitions of the term, Weakness: *"deficiency, ineffective, a fault or defect, special desire or fondness, an object of special desire or fondness."* We recognize each in the actions of those of ancient times and in ourselves today. Thankfully, God loves us enough to provide a way forward, even when we are caught in Weakness' clutches. The prophet Isaiah writes that God says to us, *"So do not fear for I am with you; … I will strengthen you and help you."* (Isaiah 41:10) The apostle Paul offers encouragement when we struggle with this foe when he writes: *"We are hard pressed on every side, but not crushed; perplexed, but not in despair; persecuted, but not abandoned; struck down, but not destroyed."* (2 Corinthians 4:7-9) And how can we forget those immortal words God spoke to the apostle after he had pleaded for release from a thorn in his flesh: *"My grace is sufficient for you, for my power is made perfect in weakness."* (2 Corinthians 12:9-10) These scriptures assure us that it was and continues to be God's grace that saves us from the snare of Weakness. He who created us knew this snare would forever plague His creation. He built into His order of the universe the plan for our redemption from it. When we in faith accept and proclaim Jesus Christ as Lord of our lives, we can walk the path to glory confidently. If our bodies begin the slide into temptation, the words in our guidebook can stay that fall. As it proclaims, *"...the Spirit helps us in our weakness. We do not know what we ought to pray for, but the Spirit himself intercedes for us."* (Romans 8:26) The word of the Lord is sufficient, for therein is His everlasting grace.

Reflection

Few of us can claim we haven't fallen from time to time into the clutches of Weakness. What's your story? When has your spirit been willing, but your body weak? What's your remedy for avoidance of this snare?

Day 25

Temptation

But watch yourself, or you may be tempted.
1 Corinthians 10:13

It's as if we hear Peter himself shouting as we round the next bend; *"Be self-controlled and alert. Your enemy the devil prowls around like a roaring lion looking for someone to devour. Resist him, standing firm in the faith."* (1 Peter 5:8-9)

We understand the urgency of his words as we approach the next pitfall: Weakness' fraternal twin—Temptation. Some of the faithful question its power considering our successfully coming to terms with Weakness a few days ago. "Aren't they one and the same?" someone asks.

We have come to understand on this walk to glory that though Weakness and Temptation share traits, the former is more a precursor for the latter; their differences manifesting in their roles. Weakness is the key that springs open the door to Temptation. Satan knew this. Scripture records in the fourth chapter of Matthew that when the Spirit led Jesus into the desert to be tempted, Satan didn't immediately confront Him. No, he waited until Jesus was weak with hunger. Figuring that His physically weaken state was the opportune time for Temptation to have its sway, Satan said, *"If you are the Son of God, tell these stones to become bread… If you are the Son of God, throw yourself down… All this I will give you if you will bow down and worship me."* (Matthew 4:4-9) Yet despite weariness in body and probably spirit, conditions that easily spawn a slide into this snare, Jesus resisted, using the word of God to counter each Temptation. In so doing He became for the faithful, both their example and their help for how to respond when Temptation threatens.

We are further reminded in our guidebook, *"No temptation has seized you except what is common to man,"* (1 Corinthians 10:13) and *"But watch yourself, or you also may be tempted."* (Galatians 6:1) We know these words speak to the human condition. How else can we explain King David's fall into Temptation's pit? Surely David knew the Ten Commandments; that the sin of adultery was common and to be avoided. Yet, despite knowing and even being counted a man after God's own heart, (1Samuel13:14) he fell prey to it. Why? The Apostle James answers, *"…but each one is tempted when, by his own evil desire, he is dragged away and enticed."* (James 1:14) What other explanation can be offered for David's actions except his submission to the desires of mind and body? *One evening David got up from his bed and walked around on the roof of the palace. From the roof, he saw a woman bathing. The woman was very beautiful, and David sent someone to find out about her. The man said, "Isn't this Bathsheba, the …wife of Uriah the Hittite?" Then David sent messengers to get her. She came to him, and he slept with her."* (2 Samuel 11:2-4)

Weakness in body, mind and spirit tempted David to commit the sin of adultery; and afterwards in his cover-up attempts, the sins of lying and murder. Did he not remember the teachings of the Torah that spoke to obeying the Ten Commandments and other Mosaic laws? *"You shall not murder. You shall not commit adultery."* (Exodus 20:13-14) Not until he was confronted with these sins by the prophet Nathan did he acknowledge his guilt: *"I have sinned against the Lord."* (2 Samuel 12:13)

Our human tendency to yield to Temptation when our bodies, minds, or spirits are weak is all too real. Desires and lust propel us to seek the very things that impede our progress on the journey. It seems we spend more time struggling to avoid Temptation than we do moving onward. Thankfully, our guidebook reminds us that we have as our constant companion the one who can sympathize with our weakness; who has been tempted in every way, just as we are, yet was without sin. (Hebrews 4:15-16) He resisted Temptation primarily by relying on the word of God. In our efforts to avoid this snare, we are well advised to do the same.

Reflection

What weaknesses spur you toward things you know you should resist? What entices you to make choices that violate biblical teachings? Do you see a connection between Weakness and Temptation, or do you consider them stand-alone pitfalls?

Day 26

STRESS

Cast your cares on the Lord and he will sustain you; he will never let the righteous fail.

Psalm 55:22

The path twists and turns such that we're struggling to keep our footing. Apparently, the adversary's ploy today is to bombard us with hassles and situations that create tension. As we stagger together, it's clear the pitfall ahead is none other than the universal disrupter of one's sense of well-being: Stress.

Stress as we know wears two faces: positive and negative. We can liken it to the ancient theatrical masks that represent tragedy and comedy. Positive Stress mimics Thalia, the upturned smiling mask. Negative Stress on the other hand is the twin of Melpomene, whose mask of tragedy is a downturned grimace. Thalia-Stress is good Stress; it is those motivating forces that propel us toward improvement and attainment of goals. Good Stress does not represent a pitfall. But the other side of the theatrical mask, the one with downturned features, represents Melpomene-Stress; the kind of Stress waiting to snare us on the journey. This negative Stress is understood to be a physical or psychological response to something that is disquieting or something that stunts our forward movement. It is not as some think, just a product of modern-day living. No, negative Stress has been part of the human condition since biblical times.

Recall Elijah's story recorded in chapter nineteen of 1 Kings. His experience is one in which Stress produced such despair that he was ready to give up living. Following a public test that demonstrated the power of God and the powerlessness of Baal, the deity worshipped by King Ahab, Elijah ordered the prophets of Baal be seized, and he killed them. (1 Kings 18:40) When Queen Jezebel heard that Elijah had slain the prophets she sent a message in which she threatened to kill him for what he had done. In fear, Elijah fled. The Stress produced by his situation drove him to a desert in Judah. *"He came to a broom tree, sat down under it and prayed that he might die. 'I have had enough,' Lord, he said. 'Take my life; I am no better than my ancestors.'"* (I Kings 19:4-5) Negative Stress took its toll; God's caring response alone saved the prophet from the desperation of his situation.

It is the same for us today. Whenever any circumstances of the human condition produce worry, anxiety, dread, or Hopelessness, God's word is our source for deliverance from the Stress produced by these spiritual demons. That is what they are, and why they have the potential to cause harm; harm that depletes us physically, emotionally, and spiritually.

Another classic example of the corrosive effects of negative Stress is found in the New Testament account of Jesus' visit in the home of the sisters, Mary and Martha. Both were obviously pleased by the Savior's visit. Martha labored in the kitchen wanting to provide exemplary hospitality. Mary sat at His feet, listening intently as He spoke. It's not difficult to imagine that as time went on, the sister in the kitchen realized she was doing all the practical work that needed to be done. We can imagine her tension building as she cooks and cleans: the tightness of her chest, a headache beginning in the back of her head, eyes blurring. Finally, the tension she feels because her sister is not helping in the preparations can't be contained and she confronts Jesus with the words: *"Lord, don't you care that my sister has left me to do the work by myself? Tell her to help me!"* (Luke 10:40) If the story were told in a comic strip, readers would laugh at this point. Oh, we all know the point of this biblical chronicle was summed up in Jesus' response. Martha was worried about things that didn't matter, while Mary understood what was important. That is surely true; but also true is the fact that tension developed in a relationship that led to Stress which affected someone in a negative manner; and eventually exploded in a verbal outburst directed at Jesus. One wonders why Martha didn't tear into Mary instead, the way sisters do when tensions between them build? Speculations aside, the point we must remember is that Stress is ever-present, lurking in the shadows ready to pounce when tension springs to life. Though the scripture doesn't record what happened after Jesus' answer, our assumption is that Martha's Stress was relieved as she allowed His words to speak to her emotional distress.

The same is true for us when we are burdened with cares that sprout negative Stress. Like Elijah and Martha, if we learn to listen to and rely upon God's counsel, we will overcome its snare. In our guidebook are the divine words of encouragement that can restore our sense of well-being when negative Stress springs up. *"For I am the Lord, your God, who takes hold of your right hand and says to you, do not fear; I will help you."* (Isaiah 41:13) *"Come to me, all who are weary and burdened, and I will give you rest."* (Matthew 11:28) *"Do not be anxious about anything, but in everything, by prayer and petition, with thanksgiving, present your requests to God. And the peace God, which transcends all understanding, will guard your hearts and your minds in Christ Jesus."* (Philippians 4:6-7) When we internalize these words and call them forth when negative Stress threatens, we will be empowered by them to avoid the pitfall.

Reflection

On a scale of one to ten, with ten representing the highest Stress level, where are you right now? What life circumstances most often produce negative Stress in you? When you are Stressed, how do you handle it? What remedies have you developed over the years to help you avoid Stress, or at least minimize its effects?

Day 27

Loneliness

The Lord goes before you; he will never leave you nor forsake you. Do not be afraid; do not be discouraged.
                                                    Deuteronomy 31:8

It's cloudy as the day breaks and we set upon the path once more. Despite the overcast, and most of us in seemingly high spirits, there are a few who appear unusually quiet and introspective. Such aberrations within the ranks typically signal an approaching pitfall. We continue, wondering as we do, what it might be. Suddenly, several of those who have been so withdrawn stop. With teary eyes and forlorn expressions, they speak to us. "We feel such despair sometimes. This journey is arduous; many with whom we began it have fallen away. And though we walk in faith, often we feel alone and afraid; that perhaps we may not endure until the end." One of our elders speaks, "Ah, so that old trick of the enemy raises its head. The pitfall of Loneliness must be just ahead."

Yes, Loneliness is a pitfall on the path to eternity. At first glance, it may not seem so. Who, after all, doesn't feel lonely at some point—a significant other leaves on a business trip for a few days, the last child heads off to college, a beloved parent or spouse dies, a friend moves across country, fellow workers turn away when you walk by or stop conversation when you enter the break room, the weekend arrives and once again you sit at home by yourself—life situations that speak to feeling solitary, but surely not stumbling blocks for the faithful.

The words of the English poet John Milton suggest otherwise, "Loneliness is the first thing which God's eye named not good." He based that assertion upon the Father's words in Genesis 2:18: *"The Lord God said, 'It is not good for the man to be alone. I will make a helper suitable for him.'"* Loneliness, that sense of desolation, or bleakness, even when you're not physically by yourself, is a snare for the believer. Loneliness can lead to discouragement; discouragement to despair and despair to quitting; giving up the goal toward which you strive—eternity with the Savior, and thereby falling headlong into the pit.

The Creator knew the potential for Loneliness to wreak havoc in the lives of those He created. Though He provided Adam his helpmate, Eve, to help combat it, throughout the eons that followed, this snare has plagued the faithful. Consider the *"man after God's own heart,"* King David. Many of the psalms he penned are expressions of his ongoing feelings of loneliness and anguish as enemies pursued him or when he suffered pangs of guilt over his own wrongdoing. We feel that Loneliness of spirit when he cries out, *"Why are you downcast, O my soul? Why so disturbed within me?"* (Psalm 42:5)

Can we forget the prophet whose moniker was "the weeping prophet?" Jeremiah, selected and charged by God to speak words of impending doom to a disobedient people, wearing a yoke around his neck no less, surely knew pangs of Loneliness. God even forbade him to marry; so, he endured alone the burden of being an outcast within his community. Even Jesus knew the emptiness of Loneliness as He prayed at Gethsemane. His followers unable to support Him in this hour of desperation, He understood for Himself God's purpose in addressing this trick of the enemy when they knelt together in creation. Even the great evangelist Paul could speak to the isolation and despair Loneliness produces: *"At my first defense, no one came to my support, but everyone deserted me."* (2 Timothy 4:16)

Yet along with these and all other accounts of Loneliness dogging the footsteps of the faithful, their words of hope and encouragement that helped them stay the course can do the same for us. *"Even though I walk through the valley of the shadow of death, I will fear no evil, you are with me; your rod and your staff, they comfort me."* (Psalm 23:4) *"Peace I leave with you; my peace I give you. I do not give to you as the world gives. Do not let your hearts be troubled and do not be afraid."* (John 14:27) *"But the Lord stood at my side and gave me strength."* (2 Timothy 4:17) Yes, Loneliness is a real and powerful threat of the enemy. But we have in hand the weapon we need to combat it. Our guidebook provides all we need to avoid this snare.

Reflection

What are your experiences with this pitfall? Are you prone to Loneliness? What circumstances bring it about? What coping mechanisms have you learned that help you combat it?

Day 28

SUFFERING

In this world you will have trouble. But take heart! I have overcome the world.

John 16:33

Conversation is uplifting today as we rejoice over the latest victory—sidestepping the snare of *Loneliness*. For easier access, most of us have begun keeping our guidebook in hand, not in our backpacks; and in so doing are finding ourselves more engaged in the Word. A fellow traveler is reading aloud from Psalm 30, *"O Lord my God, I called to you for help and you healed me... you spared me from going down into the pit."* Her lyrical cadence of David's song of praise and deliverance is timely as we make our way around the bend in the road and see the pitfall, Suffering, opening on the path ahead.

Even before Jesus told His followers they would experience trouble in the world (John 16:33), the sting of Suffering was common to the human experience. The sagas of this snare have dotted the landscape wherever people walked, and whether self or other inflicted, Suffering is as much a surety as death and taxes. Typically, the biblical ancestor we lift as an example of what it means to suffer is Job, the righteous man whom God allowed to suffer unbelievable tragedy and loss. But there were others who knew the pain and hurt of this pitfall; who were consumed by it in ways we find difficult to understand.

Consider the prophet Hosea, whom God told to marry a prostitute, as a way to symbolize the message He was sending to Israel regarding the nation's unfaithfulness. Gomer's escapades of promiscuity were probably common knowledge in the community. We can only imagine the talk at the water-well when the women came to fill their jars; and the whispers of the men gathered in small groups throughout town. Yet despite the humiliation of being married to Gomer in the first place, and then having to take her back after she deserted him for another man, Hosea did as God directed. In a time and culture when the punishment for her behavior would have called for stoning until death, Hosea simply endured the hurt and pain of her unfaithfulness. In Hosea's story of "other-inflicted" Suffering, he did not abandon his belief in the Father. Like Job, Hosea's trust in God's omnipotence and omniscience helped him stay the course of the faithful.

In the New Testament of our guidebook we see Suffering continuing to cast its net. During his three-year ministry, Jesus knew intimately the pangs of Suffering: rejection by the community in which He grew to manhood, homelessness, false accusations, loneliness, hunger, sadness, death of close friends, denial and betrayal by His closest companions, and the ultimate Suffering of crucifixion. But He allowed none of these misfortunes to deter His purpose: Suffering for humankind's salvation. He defeated the pitfall with the eternal cry of the faithful, *"… yet not my will, but yours be done."* (Luke 22:42)

In the years following Jesus' resurrection, our biblical forefathers and mothers continued to know Suffering as part and parcel of the human condition. Recall the travails of the disciples and apostles as they spread the gospel throughout the regions of that time. Our sense of the Sufferings they endured for their faith is epitomized in the life Paul: threats of death, trials, imprisonment, and shipwreck. It's true today few of the faithful experience these extremes, but all have met Suffering in some form or another—sickness, inequality, mistreatment, losses of all kind. The list is as long the line of believers with whom we journey. But our guidebook is open; and we are empowered with its words of assurance to navigate around the snares of this pitfall: *"The Lord is good, a refuge in times of trouble. He cares for those who trust in him."* (Nahum 1:7) *"A righteous man may have many troubles, but the Lord delivers him from them all."* (Psalm 34:19) *"We are hard pressed on every side, but not crushed; perplexed, but not in despair; persecuted, but not abandoned; struck down, but not destroyed."* (2 Corinthians 4:8-9) *"Because he loves me,"* says the Lord, *"I will rescue him; I will protect him, for he acknowledges my name. He will call upon me, and I will answer him; I will be with him in trouble, I will deliver him and honor him. With long life will I satisfy him and show him my salvation."* (Psalm 91:14-16)

Reflection

What are your thoughts as you consider Suffering as a pitfall? How might it snare you? Or sway you away from your journey? What Suffering have you endured that truly tested your faith? Or made you question God? What enabled you to hold on to your faith?

Day 29

Revenge

It is mine to avenge; I will repay.

Deuteronomy 32:35

The new day dawns and we pick up the pace to distance ourselves from that last snare. The words of our guidebook along with personal stories of overcoming *Sufferings* of various kinds helped. But there were a few folks who felt that wasn't enough, especially if *Suffering* has been caused by someone else's actions. The proverbial "eye for an eye and tooth for a tooth" captures their sentiments. As the temperature of the discussion rises, we're not surprised when the pitfall, Revenge, comes into view.

It's easy to see why the Revenge snare follows that of *Suffering*. At some point in life we all suffer pain or harm inflicted (intentionally or not) upon us by another. When that happens, it can give rise to a spirit of vengeance; that sprite who resides in the recesses of our being, waiting when provoked to spring into action. Was that not at the heart of the Cain and Abel story? Recall God's warning to Cain in the fourth chapter of the book of Genesis. He was angry at his brother Abel for reasons over which Abel had no control.

Seeking to forestall retribution having its way, God said to Cain, *"Why are you angry?... sin is crouching at your door; it desires to have you."* Cain's desire for vengeance led to the first homicide recorded in the Bible. At that decisive moment, Revenge stepped from the shadows and secured its place in the annals of pitfalls.

Stories of retribution for grievances abound in the Bible, in literary works, on our televisions, electronic devices, and theater screens where the siren of the cinema calls. When Jacob's daughter Dinah is raped by a Hivite prince, her brothers devise a scheme of Revenge for this violation of their sister, which results in the slaughter of all the males of the town. (Genesis 34) When the prophet Elijah has all the prophets of Baal killed following a showdown on Mount Carmel, Queen Jezebel vows Revenge against him. He is forced to flee to escape her proclamation of retribution. (1 Kings 18-19) Few of us leave high school or college without some degree of exposure to Shakespeare's "Hamlet," the famous play of a son's desire for Revenge for the death of his father. Alexander Dumas' intriguing tale, "The Count of Monte Cristo," is yet another example of Revenge plotted for grievances. In print and on the cinema screen this story follows the methodical retribution an innocent man devises for the three persons responsible for the years he spent in prison. Countless numbers of us were mesmerized over forty years ago as we watched Michael Corleone's Revenge for the deaths of his father and brother unfold in graphically brutal details in the iconic movie, "The Godfather," by Francis Ford Coppola?

Yes, the desire for Revenge or retaliation for injustices is as much a snare today as it was in ages past. Its manifestation plays out wherever people, their passions, perceptions, and perspectives collide. Both the breaking news and evening recaps give us daily glimpses of mankind's desire to get even, to give tit-for-tat, to not turn the other cheek, to exact vengeance for perceived wrongs. But our guidebook that details God's blueprint calls believers to a profoundly different mindset.

Who set the gold standard in the Old Testament for reacting to wrongs perpetrated by others? Great question. The answer: Joseph, the son of Jacob. The victim of his brothers' jealousy, Joseph had every reason to seek Revenge; but the fiftieth chapter of Genesis shows us the better way. Joseph spoke to the brothers who had spitefully mistreated and wronged him these timeless words: *"You intended to harm me, but God intended it for good to accomplish what is now being done."* In the New Testament, Peter speaks plainly when he writes, *"Do not repay evil for evil or insult with insult, but with blessing..."* and adds, *"... seek peace and pursue it."* (1 Peter 3:8-12) Further counsel is offered by the Apostle Paul when he writes, *"Make sure nobody pays back wrong for wrong,"* (1 Thessalonians 5:15) and *"Bless those who persecute you; bless and do not curse. Do not repay anyone evil for evil. Do not take revenge, my friends, but leave room for God's wrath, for it is written, 'It is mine to avenge; I will repay,'* says the Lord."* (Romans 12:14-19) With these words in mind, we are able to resist the pull of Revenge, and make our way around its snare.

Reflections

Since you committed to this path to glory, how often have you come upon this pitfall? What experiences have sent you into the fury of vengeful thinking? Can you recall a time when you have been the victim of wrongdoing? What redress, if any, did you seek?

Day 30

ANXIETY

When anxiety was great within me, your consolation brought joy to my soul.

Psalm 94:19

We collectively praise God as the day's journey commences. By His grace and with His word we have turned aside yet another pitfall on our path, and though we wish we could be done with these snares, we understand that mastering the terrain upon which they lay in wait is germane to reaching our goal. Still, some trepidation is apparent as we move forward. We discover its source when the pitfall of Anxiety comes into view.

Some seasoned saints may recall the lyrics of an old African American hymn the faithful sang in times of tribulation: "When *I'm troubled, Lord, walk with me. All along my pilgrim journey, Lord, I want Jesus to walk with me.*" The fact of their faith did not spare these believers life experiences which caused Anxiety and summoned these plaintive words. And as scripture teaches, neither were our biblical ancestors immune to the attributes of Anxiety's pitfall: fearful concerns, apprehensive uneasiness, worry. The only man recorded as knowing

God face to face, Moses, danced around its perimeter. When God told him, he was to go to the Egyptian Pharaoh and bring out the people held in bondage, Anxiety seized him. *"Who am I that I should go to Pharaoh and bring the Israelites out of Egypt?"* was his first response. (Exodus 3:10-11) His uneasiness and fear of doing what God wanted him to do escalated into fearful excuse after excuse until the Bible says God's anger burned against Moses. (Exodus 4:14) Even the mighty King Saul knew great Anxiety when he heard the challenging boast of the Philistine Goliath. *"On hearing the Philistine's words, Saul and the Israelites were dismayed and terrified."* (1 Samuel 17:11) And what can account for the behavior of the disciples hiding behind locked doors following Jesus' crucifixion except great fear and Anxiety over their own plight? (John 20:19)

The quivering feeling of Anxiety knows no age or time frame. Whether in the guise of youthful worries related to mundane issues, or more adult complexities in our modern world, Anxiety shadows our steps. Because it is so pervasive, we often feel we are unable to resist its pull. It's as if we've adapted to a motto of, "Got Anxiety? Live with it." But for those of us serious about this journey of faith, the guidebook suggests there is an alternative mindset. The psalmist proclaims we can cast our cares on the Lord and he will sustain us and never let the righteous fall. (Psalm 55:22) In another instance, he writes, *"God is our refuge and strength, an ever-present help in trouble. Therefore, we will not fear."* (Psalm 46:2-4) That stalwart apostle of the faith, Paul, tells us, *"Do not be anxious about anything, but in everything, by prayer and petition, with thanksgiving, present your requests to God."* (Philippians 4:6)

In his writings to believers throughout the world, the apostle Peter pens *"Cast all your anxiety on him because he cares for you."* (1 Peter 5:7) Jesus Himself offers us even more defenses against the peril of this pitfall in the Gospel of Matthew. In His sermon on a mountainside, He spoke, *"Therefore, I tell you, do not worry about your life."* (Matthew 6:25) At another time, He offered these words of encouragement, *"Come to me, all you who are wearied and burdened, and I will give you rest."* (Matthew 11:28) Perhaps our most powerful "go-to" scripture when Anxiety threatens is found in the Gospel of John: *"Peace I leave with you; my peace I give to you. I do not give to you as the world gives. Do not let your hearts be troubled and do not be afraid."* (John 14:27) With these affirmations, we can cast aside any lingering trepidation and triumphantly step over yet another potential pitfall.

Reflection

What common anxieties keep you awake at night or cloud your day with worry, uneasiness or fear? How do you drive them away?

Day 31

AMBITION

Do nothing out of selfish ambition or vain conceit, but in humility consider others better than yourselves.

Philippians 2:3

We rejoice as the sun rises on a new day. We take on Paul's mindset and forget what lies behind us, determined to press forward as the path stretches ahead. Our guidebook has become a welcomed walking cane. Leaning on it provides the wisdom needed to avoid falling into the path's many snares. Today, once again, its value is proven as we approach the ambiguous pitfall of Ambition. Some fellow travelers declare it's not a pitfall at all; and are ready to offer evidence to support their claim. But others shake their heads in disagreement.

The dictionary defines Ambition as "desire for rank, fame, or power; desire for personal achievement or preferment; inordinate (immoderate, excessive, exceeding reasonable limits) desire." The Apostle Paul's exhortation noted in the day's scripture seems to support this meaning of the term. We have only to look within the guidebook for further confirmation. Was not Adam and Eve's decision to eat from the tree of knowledge nothing more than a desire to possess the same power God had? (Genesis 3) What else but desire for fame and personal achievement led to the building of the Tower of Babel? (Genesis 4) What, other than selfish Ambition, led the remnant of the Israelites to build houses for themselves, before constructing God's house as written in the book of Haggai? Even during Jesus' ministry, some of His followers revealed the danger of this pitfall as they argued about who was the greatest among them. (Mark 9:33-37) As He teaches His disciples, Jesus defines greatness not as preferment or personal achievement, but denial of self and putting God first. He asks one of the defining questions of our faith, *"What good will it be for a man if he gains the whole world, yet forfeits his soul?"* (Matthew 16:21-27)

Even literature abounds with stories of Ambition, excessiveness, desires that exceed reasonableness, that proved perilous to those who tumbled into the snare. Recall the mythological character, Phaeton, whose Ambition to drive the sun chariot for a day led to natural disaster and his death. Or Shakespeare's Macbeth, whose character flaw of Ambition led to his downfall. Theater goers may recall the main character, Willie Loman, in "Death of a Salesman." His all-consuming Ambition for the achievement of wealth yielded not success, but destruction. Perhaps our best non-biblical account of Ambition gone awry is found in John Milton's "Paradise Lost." This story of the fall of man and Satan tells of Satan's Ambition to overthrow God. His desire for power drives him to wage war against the Almighty; a war he lost, as he did his place in heaven when God cast him out.

As we stand on the brink of Ambition's pitfall, someone adds a 20th century account of the destructiveness of

Ambition: The Holocaust. Another reminds us that Ambition can have a positive side. She points to mankind's progress in many areas that would not have happened if a spirit of Ambition had not spurred individuals to pursue certain goals: Martin Luther King Jr. and The Civil Rights Movement, Mother Teresa and Mahatma Gandhi, reform efforts in child labor, women's rights, and a host of others that demonstrate Ambition's positive attributes. Yes, we conclude, Ambition is ambiguous. When its genesis is unselfish desire rooted in humility that looks to the needs and interests of others, we may discern it to be positive. But if its origin springs from the well of preferment and advancement of one's own desires at the expense of others, it is a snare to be avoided.

Reflection

What's your take on this pitfall? Is it a snare or not? What about you? Would you describe yourself as ambitious? What would others say about you in this regard? Is Ambition a trait the faithful should nurture or quell?

Day 32

Complaining

Do everything without complaining or arguing so that you may become blameless and pure...
                                      Philippians 2:14-16

It's somewhat overcast this morning as we set upon today's portion of the pathway to glory. The twists and turns we see ahead are causing consternation. A believer asks aloud, *"Why is the path always so crooked? Aren't we supposed to be on a straight path to heaven? We've committed to following Jesus, so why are we still dealing with so many obstacles along the way?"* As has become the custom now whenever such questions arise, we open the guidebook for answers; and immediately discern the pitfall we approach is aptly named, Complaining.

One of our biblical scholars takes us back to the Garden of Eden to illustrate that Complaining, or one of its companions—grumbling, protesting, whining, carping, and grousing—has played a role in the relationship between God and humans since the beginning. When God confronted Adam and Eve with their disobedience, what was Adam's response? He complained via protest. *"The woman you put here with me—she gave me some fruit from the tree and I ate it."*

(Genesis 3:12) In other words, *it's not my fault. If you hadn't put the woman here with me, I would not have disobeyed you.* Seemingly mankind's default position of Complaining was an inborn behavior from the onset.

Even the Lord's intervention to deliver His people from the bondages of slavery in Egypt and shepherd them through the wilderness to a promised land did not squelch their proclivity toward Complaining. *"Now the people complained about their hardships in the hearing of the Lord; and when he heard them his anger was roused."* (Numbers 11:1) During his years of trying to lead the Israelites as God had instructed him, Moses too gave in to Complaining. He directed his carping directly at God. *"Why have you brought this trouble on your servant?... I cannot carry all these people by myself; the burden is too heavy for me."* (Numbers 11:10-15) The human penchant for Complaining touched even the great king and psalmist David. How often have we read that great cry of complaint in Psalm 22, *"My God, my God, why have you forsaken me? Why are you so far from saving me, so far from the words of my groaning?"* We recall in Jesus' time on earth the grousing of Martha because Mary sat at the Savior's feet rather than assisting her sister with preparations in the kitchen. *"Lord, don't you care that my sister has left me to do the work by myself? Tell her to help me!"* (Luke 10:40)

Yes, Complaining, the expression of dissatisfaction about something or a statement of suffering or grievance, is common to us all. We complain about numberless things: the weather—*too hot, too cold, too rainy, too dry*; our jobs when we have them and lack thereof when we don't; family members; friends; church folk; politicians; the state of the world; the economy; taxes and prices for goods and services; crime;

ethnic and religious intolerance; all the "isms" and injustices. In fact, it seems we expend an inordinate amount of time and energy in complaint mode, often as a defense of our actions. In truth, there are certainly issues worthy of our protest; that demand protest. But setting those issues aside, far too many of us complain too often for too many reasons that are unworthy of us as believers. Paul's counsel in our day's scripture reminds us that the growth in the qualities of blamelessness and purity that we seek as Christians is tied to lessening our Complaining, grumbling and arguing.

If we reflect for a moment on our call as Christ followers, we must accept that moments and issues that lend themselves to Complaining are ones that test our faith. Consider such a time for the prophet Habakkuk when it seemed God had turned a deaf ear his prayers: *"How long, O Lord, must I call for help, but you do not listen? Or cry out to you, 'Violence!' but you do not save?"* (Habakkuk 1:1-2) This moment of Complaining was surely a test of Habakkuk's faith. Would his unanswered prayers lead to disillusionment with God? Quite the opposite, as we see in his proclamation later, *"Though the fig tree does not bud and there are no grapes on the vines, though the olive crop fails and the fields produce no food, though there are no sheep in the pen and no cattle in the stalls, yet I will rejoice in the Lord, I will be joyful in God my Savior."* (Habakkuk 3:17-18)

On this perilous path to glory we have the benefit of such examples of biblical ancestors to guide us. James advises, *"Don't grumble against each other."* (James 5:9) Yes, the human tendency to complain is ever present, and yielding to it is what the enemy desires. But not this time. One by one we step around this pitfall, shedding all remnants of a Complaining spirit as we stride forward.

Reflection

Are you a Complainer? How would those who know you best answer that question? What are you more likely to whine or complain about as it relates to your personal or professional life? If you are a member of Complainers Anonymous, what steps can you take to break the habit?

Day 33

ADDICTION

Everything is permissible for me, but I will not be mastered by anything.

1 Corinthians 6:12

As the day begins, we settle again into the rhythm of the journey. We've come to expect the path to offer snares; and from this point onward, we know one will pop up at any given moment. For a while we proceed in peaceful contemplation. Then we hear the growingly familiar words from a believer further ahead, *"Watch out! I see the next pitfall; it's* Addiction, *and it's huge."* No one cringes at this warning; instead with confidence, all open the guidebook.

Addiction, as the dictionary defines the word, is the fact or condition of being dependent upon a substance, thing, or activity. In other words, Addiction can be considered an obsession with, mania, or passion for, or enslavement to something that overpowers one's ability to make wise choices, and contrary to popular opinion, it is not new to the human experience. Centuries before its primary depiction of those seeking the next fix of their drug of choice, the pitfall of Addiction has long served the enemy's relentless assault upon believers. It is indeed huge, as its tentacles of sex, food, drink, envy, power, to name but a few, demonstrate how difficult it is to avoid.

During what we know as the Bronze Age, and our earliest recordings of biblical history during this time, we glimpse the snare of sexual Addiction's immortality in the account of destruction of the cities of Sodom and Gomorrah. (Genesis 19:1-5) That those misguided sexual passions would encourage addictive behaviors is not an unreasonable assumption for God's sixth commandment: *"You shall not commit adultery."* (Exodus 20:14) What other than the pitfall of Addiction can explain King David's behavior as he watched another man's wife bathe? Yielding to his sexual passions explains his subsequent sin of adultery. (2 Samuel 11) In the writings of Solomon, we read admonition after admonition against sexual Addiction in the form of adultery and the addictive harms of alcohol that lead to drunkenness.

Truly our tendency toward Addiction's pitfall is long standing, stretching from the recorded times of 2,300 BC to the present. Today we sense its seeming invincibility as Addictions of sex, food, drink, drugs, envy, power, gambling, etc. touch us or others. Paul's conundrum speaks to the power of this pitfall, *"I do not understand what I do. For what I want to do I do not do, but what I hate I do."* (Romans 7:15) And though the destructiveness of the Addiction pitfall appears overwhelming, we are not helpless to stand against it.. In our guidebook, we have the words of our biblical ancestors to call upon for hope and encouragement. In Romans 6:11-14, Paul writes, *"Therefore do not let sin reign in your mortal body so that you obey its evil desires. Do not offer the parts of your body to sin, as instruments of wickedness, but rather offer yourselves to God... For sin shall not be your master."* He continues this advice on countering Addiction's pitfall in chapter twelve when he reminds us that our body is a living sacrifice, and we are not to conform to the world. In Philippians, chapters three and four, he says we surrender to Addiction when we allow our stomach to be our god and occupy our minds with earthly things.

Paul further instructs in the letter to the church in Corinth, that the believer must not be mastered by food, sex, or anything else, but honor God with his body and his mind. When we can learn to follow these sound words of counsel, the darkness of another pitfall will fade away. Our path will clear, and unscathed we will continue the journey. Our collective prayer is that this will be the case sooner than later.

Reflection

Think. Are there things to which you are addicted, aside from chocolate (and that too is suspect if it's contributing to body fat issues)? Seriously, what are you so passionate or obsessive about that it might meet the litmus test of an Addiction? Is addiction ever okay? Explain your thoughts and rationale.

Day 34

Failure

For all have sinned and fall short of the glory of God.
Romans 3:23-24

As we all skirt around that last pitfall, leaving it in the dust so to speak, some of the travelers appear somber despite our triumph. Their solemn attitude is puzzling until the path takes a turn, and we see ahead the next impediment on the journey: the pitfall Failure. We immediately recognize why this pitfall follows Addiction. Often it is Failure to resist addictive behaviors and maintain sobriety in living our faith that hurls us into the clutches of this newest snare. At other times it springs to entangle us when we attempt to do what we perceive as righteous and fail. And sometimes we fall prey to it simply because we sin.

Since the beginning of time, mankind has known what it means to fail, i.e., to experience defeat, disaster, or catastrophe; for success to be elusive, to know the hollow feeling of one's best efforts resulting in collapse or fiasco. Consider a few of our biblical ancestors and how they both encountered and resisted this snare of the enemy. Jacob's son Joseph created such a rift with his older brothers that they sold him into slavery. Though the ensuing consequences of their actions could have plunged Joseph into this pit, it did not. As the years passed, he held to his faith convictions and allowed God to use him in ways that blessed others. That paragon of unmerited disaster, Job, knew firsthand the frustration of having one's best intentions go awry. Despite his righteous living, disaster struck and he lost everything; except the wife who told him to curse God and die. But as we know, he did just the opposite. In the throes of Failure, Job refused to throw in the towel; instead he pronounced victory over Failure with the proclamation, *"The Lord gave and the Lord has taken away; may the name of the Lord be praised."* (Job 1:21) And how can we forget the disciple Peter who failed miserably when the going got rough. After denying he knew Jesus three times at the rooster's third crow, Peter felt the bitterness of his Failure and he broke down and wept. (Mark 14:72) Yet the sorrow of his betrayal could not hold him for long. His bold witness of faith in the Savior before the crowd gathered at Pentecost shed any lingering tentacles of the Failure pitfall.

These are but a few of the examples of those who stayed the course on their journey, and because we are not immune to Failure, they offer us hope. Many carry the weight of recidivism; of turning back to habits and practices that negate the profession of faith. Some suffer physical and emotional traumas that test the possession of faith when they go unresolved. Others flirt with resignation when righteousness does not yield the fulfillment of God's promises. But in these, and all circumstances that threaten to push us into Failure's snare, we have the resource with which to resist the enemy. Proverbs 24:16-18 reminds us, *"for though a righteous man falls seven times, he rises again."* Psalm 145:14-16 offers encouragement when Failure beckons, *"The Lord upholds all those who fall and lifts up all who are bowed down."* The writer of Hebrews pens, *"You need to persevere so that when you have done the will of God, you will receive what he has promised."* (Hebrews 10:36) The words of Habakkuk ring with hope for the times when it seems everything is lost and Failure has won: *"Though the fig tree does not bud and there are no grapes on the vine, though the olive crop fails and the fields produce not food, though there are no sheep in the pen and no cattle in the stalls, yet I will rejoice in the Lord, I will be joyful in God my Savior."* (Habakkuk 3:17-18)

As these words filter through the ranks, those with slumping shoulders and grim countenances begin to stand straighter and somber expressions fade from their faces. With the rest of us, they maneuver around the Failure pitfall and stride purposefully onward.

Reflection

We all fail at one time or another, for one reason or another. Think of times in your life when Failure has tapped on your shoulder and you've danced for a while in its embrace. What kept you from remaining in its clutches? What advice can you offer those who stand now at its precipice? Are there positives to failing? Explain your perspective.

Day 35

Prosperity

Jesus looked at him and loved him. "One thing you lack," he said. "Go, sell everything you have and give to the poor, and you will have treasure in heaven. Then come, follow me." At this the man's face fell. He went away sad, because he had great wealth… "How hard it is for the rich to enter the kingdom of God."

Mark 10:21-23

The path has been uneventful and unusually smooth for a while. A sense of well-being hovers over us. In fact, we haven't felt this confident since we began the journey. Little do we realize that this sense of *all is well* is but a precursor of the adversary's next snare. And just as the deceiver tries to wrap us in his cloak of success, we come upon it. Stretching across our path in all its faux-glitter is the pitfall of Prosperity. "Wait a minute," a fellow traveler calls out. "Why is Prosperity considered a snare? Scripture seems to suggest otherwise. It informs us that *Misfortune pursues the sinner, but prosperity is the reward of the righteous;* and *A greedy man stirs up dissension, but he who trusts in the Lord will prosper.*" (Proverbs 13:21 and 28:25 respectively) Understandably our pace slows as we reflect upon those scriptures. Unseen in the shadows, the enemy is gleeful; he delights in confusion amongst believers, as he knows it is the slippery slope before the plunge.

Thankfully, an elder's voice rises above the disjointed chatter. "In and of itself," the elder intones, "Prosperity—the condition of being successful or thriving, having economic wellbeing—is not a snare. It becomes one when believers make it a god, something that turns them away from trusting the source of Prosperity, God Himself." He opens the guidebook. We listen as he begins to read scriptures that expose the inherent danger of what we are facing. *"If I have put my trust in gold or said to pure gold, 'You are my security,' If I have rejoiced over my great wealth, the fortune my hands had gained… then these also would be sins to be judged, for I would have been unfaithful to God on high."* (Job: 31:24-28) Continuing, he draws our attention to Luke 12:13-21. Jesus was teaching the crowd when someone said to him, *"Teacher, tell my brother to divide the inheritance with me."* Though disclaiming that He is an arbiter in this dispute, Jesus uses it to warn against the dangers of greed, abundance, and material possessions. He tells the story of a rich man so prosperous, he had no place even to store what he owned. He decided to tear down his barns and build bigger ones for his goods, saying to himself, *"You have plenty of good things laid up for many years. Take life easy; eat, drink and be merry."* But God burst that bubble of trust in his Prosperity: *"You fool! This very night your life will be demanded from you. Then who will get what you have prepared for yourself? This is how it will be for anyone who stores up things for himself but is not rich toward God."*

This is Prosperity's dark side, the yawning pitfall on the path to eternity. The writer of Hebrews counsels us to avoid it by keeping our lives free from the love of money, and being content with what we have; for such an attitude confirms our trust in God who has told us, *"Never will I leave you; never will I forsake you."* (Hebrews 13:5) And because Prosperity is equated with economic success, the Apostle Paul's warning is relevant to avoiding this trick of the enemy. He writes, *"People who want to get rich fall into temptation and a trap and into many foolish and harmful desires that plunge men into ruin and destruction. For the love of money is a root of all kinds of evil. Some people, eager for money, have wandered from the faith…"* (1 Timothy 6:9-10)

The desire for Prosperity is not uncommon; few turn from its perks. Often, we recall the words of Jeremiah to justify our desire for it: *"For I know the plans I have for you, declares the Lord, plans to prosper you."* (Jeremiah 29:11) If God desires to prosper us, we say, then what's the danger of Prosperity, the outcome of His prospering? The answer gets us to the crux of this issue. God's concept of Prosperity is not worldly; it is not measured by our bank accounts, the neighborhoods we live in, the model of the car we drive, or whether we wear designer-labeled clothing. Rather, God's Prosperity abides in the spiritual realm and the fruits therein. Spiritual prospering is measured by the amount of love we show and joy we possess in our relationships with others; it is calculated by the models of patience, kindness, gentleness, and goodness we allow to transport us throughout the day; it is counted by our faithfulness in following Jesus' command to do unto others as we would have them do to us, in our neighborhood and beyond; and it is assessed by the self-control we wear daily in adherence to the Master's call. These attributes of the spirit are the underpinnings of God's Prosperity. When we possess them, we live in right relationship with the Father and place our trust in Him. Unlike material Prosperity that fades and decays, spiritual Prosperity will last until eternity. Seeking it, rather than the riches of the world, will bring the treasures God desires for us. Perhaps the Apostle Paul offers the definitive message regarding this pitfall when he writes, *"Command those who are rich in this present world not to be arrogant nor to put their hope in wealth, which is so uncertain, but to put their hope in God."* (1 Timothy 6:17)

Reflection

Do you struggle with this pitfall? What is your understanding of Prosperity? Is it benign or a danger to the believer on the path to glory? What are your thoughts on the current Prosperity gospel preached in some churches today?

Day 36

Lust

Do not love the world or anything in the world. If anyone loves the world, the love of the Father is not in him. For everything in the world—the cravings of sinful man, the lust of his eyes and the boasting of what he has and does—comes not from the Father but from the world.

                                            1 John 2:15-16

Reassembled for today's leg of the journey, we speak softly about the last pitfall and its potential to deter us from our goal. These snares of the enemy are sharpening our sense of what it means to be faithful (surely not the Devil's intent). With each encounter, we shed more of the naiveté that marked us when we began this journey. The guidebook, God's Word, is proving to be as the psalmist writes, "*… a lamp to my feet and a light for my path.*" (Psalm 119:105) The more we partake of its wisdom, the less threatening the obstacles we meet. The next pitfall, Lust, is not unfamiliar. We approach it armed with our Spirit sword. And though the perimeter is slippery, and we stumble a bit, we are determined to not fall prey to its tentacles.

Long held by Christian tradition as one of the Seven

Deadly Sins, Lust is defined as an uncontrollable passion or longing, especially for sexual desires. As with the other six transgressions, Lust can be fatal to the believer's spiritual progress. With its scarlet banner billowing above the pitfall, it weaves a web of ardor and desire beginning in the mind or heart and then manifesting—unless checked—in damning behaviors. The writer of Proverbs cautions against Lusting in the heart for a woman's beauty (Proverbs 6:25); similar warnings against forbidden sexual desires are sprinkled throughout the Mosaic laws. Surely adherence to those laws would have saved King David from his entanglement in this web.

The story of his plunge is immortalized in 2 Samuel 11:1-12. In our mind's eye, we see him as he gazes too long upon a woman bathing on the rooftop of her home across from the palace. She captivates him, and as the scripture reads, *"The woman was very beautiful, and David sent someone to find out about her. The man said, 'Isn't this Bathsheba ... the wife of Uriah the Hittite?'"* Oh, had but David at this moment, remembering the teachings of his forefathers, turned away, this epic tale of Lust might never have been written. But sin had already taken root where it usually does—in the heart. And David, seemingly with little thought, yields to the desires of the flesh. *"Then David sent messengers to get her. She came to him, and he slept with her."* We know the rest of the story; how one sin begat another and another, until the prophet Nathan stood before the king and confronted him with his transgressions.

The power of Lust to impede the Christian's journey is perhaps why Jesus taught, *"You have heard it said, 'Do not commit adultery.' But I tell you that anyone who looks at a woman lustfully has already committed adultery with her in his heart."* (Matthew 5:27-28) In several of his epistles to the churches and believers struggling to both remain faithful and grow in faith, the Apostle Paul echoed Jesus' admonitions against sexual Lust. *"Do not commit adultery… Let us behave decently, not in sexual immorality… Put to death, therefore, whatever belongs to your earthly nature: sexual immorality… lust… that each of you should learn to control his own body in a way that is holy and honorable, not in passionate lust."* (Romans 13:8-14; Colossians 3:5; 1 Thessalonians 4:5)

Our guidebook has once again empowered us with what we need to counter this pitfall; and we're almost passed it when someone asks, "But doesn't Lust extend to more than just sexual desires? Shouldn't we be careful of its guises in other areas of our life?" The collective nods of affirmation cause us to slow our pace. Someone reads aloud the words of today's scripture: *"For everything in the world—the cravings of sinful man, the lust of his eyes and the boasting of what he has and does—comes not from the Father but from the world."* With broaden perspective, we grasp that Lust, beyond its sexual connotation, encompasses anything we fervently crave more than we should. Our longing for material possessions and other markers of position or power rank second on the infamous Lust List. They are the things about which we boast and place our identity. They are the desires that shift our focus from God to the world. We reflect upon man's definition of a life well-lived. Is it the life of the person who seeks to live in right relationship with God and in obedience to his Word, or the life of one whose primary quests are for wealth, power, fame; and the accolades the world gives for those achievements?

In sober tones, some believers share that they initially felt this pitfall was not one in which they would be snared. But the guidebook expanded their understanding of its deceptiveness. Now we all see Lust from more than the lens of sexual immorality. Our vision is widened. We grasp it as idolatry and a violation of the first commandment to have no other god before God. That is what lust is: desire for anything more than the desire for God.

Reflection

What was your first understanding of this pitfall? Has your understanding changed? Is Lust a challenge you face, or have ever faced?

Day 37

Favoritism

My brothers, as believers in our glorious Lord Jesus Christ, don't show favoritism.

James 2:1

Grateful again for the guidance our guidebook is providing, we return to the path with renewed purpose. Someone remarks that the pitfalls seem to be less threatening now than when we began this trek to glory. Many disagree and suggest that the snares can't really be measured in terms of difficulty. All of them have the potential to impede our journey, and as such pose a hazard to our spiritual well-being. We agree we cannot afford to give the enemy the slightest loophole; the very pitfall that on the surface might appear harmless can be the one that snares us. All too soon that proves true as the pitfall of Favoritism opens wide before us.

Two stories of the harm caused by Favoritism are told early in our biblical history. As Isaac and Rebekah's twin sons, Esau and Jacob, grew, Scripture records: *"… Esau became a skilled hunter, a man of the open country, while Jacob was a quiet man, staying among the tents. Isaac, who had a taste for wild game, loved Esau, but Rebekah loved Jacob."* (Genesis 25:27-28) Rebekah's partiality for Jacob prompted their sin of deceit committed in order for him to receive the blessing intended for his older brother. *"Jacob said to his father, 'I am Esau your firstborn.'"* (Genesis 27:19) And with that lie, planted by his mother's Favoritism, ill-feelings between the brothers sprouted into animosity that forever tainted their relationship. Years later when the brothers had a reconciliatory meeting, Jacob was plagued still by his deception and its consequences; and presumably out of fear of Esau's rightful retaliation, moved not to Seir to live near him, but to the land of Succoth. (Genesis 33)

Perhaps the more familiar story of Favoritism and its subsequent harms is that of Joseph, Jacob's son born to him in his later years. *"Now Israel (Jacob) loved Joseph more than any of his other sons... and he made a richly ornamented robe for him. When his brothers saw that their father loved him more than any of them, they hated him."* (Genesis 37:3-4) Not only did apparent parental Favoritism cause a major rift between siblings, but it also gave rise to Joseph's inflated sense of who was in relationship to his family. After all, if your daddy thinks you *hung the moon*, then surely you must be special. Why else would you have dreams of the *"sun and moon and eleven stars bowing down to you?"* (Genesis 37:9) We know of course that God moves in His own way to bring about His purposes; and not even Jacob's time in this pitfall could alter His ultimate plans. Yet for a time, Favoritism had its way and proved its destructiveness.

This snare is not consigned to just Old Testament writings. Dotted throughout the New Testament are various warnings against it. In the book of Acts, Peter speaks. *"I now realize how true it is that God does not show favoritism but accepts men from every nation who fear him and do what is right."* (Acts 10:34) The Apostle Paul speaks to Favoritism in several epistles. *"For God does not show favoritism." (Romans 2:11) "Anyone who does wrong will be repaid for his wrong, and there is no favoritism."* (Colossians 3:25*) "... keep these instructions without partiality... and do nothing out of favoritism."* (1 Timothy 5:21) And the Apostle James writes forcibly, *"If you really keep the royal law found in Scripture 'Love your neighbor as yourself,' you are doing right. But if you show favoritism, you sin and are convicted by the law as lawbreakers."* (James 2:8-9)

Finally, we have only to look at the life of our Savior to understand that showing Favoritism is not a behavior worthy of those committed to following Him. Jesus was not selective in His ministry; He showed Favoritism toward no one, irrespective of position or status, ethnicity, gender, or religion. He ministered to all He encountered in the three and half years he modeled what it means to be a disciple. Levi and Zacchaeus, the tax collectors; Jairus, a synagogue leader; a Roman centurion; a demon-possessed man; a rich ruler; the Samaritan woman at the well; or Nicodemus, a member of the Jewish ruling council—Jesus' encounters with each speak to the diversity of His ministry and its lack of Favoritism. Jesus is inclusive; He does not give preferential treatment to a person at the expense of another. Whenever we do, and are unfair or biased, we stray from the path and are easy prey for the tentacles of the pitfall, Favoritism.

Reflection

Is avoidance of this pitfall easy or hard? Explain your thoughts. Are there times when showing Favoritism is acceptable? Do you see it as a major or minor concern for the believer in Jesus Christ?

Day 38

SELFISHNESS

Turn my heart toward your statues, and not toward selfish gain.

Psalm 119:36

As the morning dawns, we fix our eyes on the path, wondering what this day might bring. Gone is the expectation that we'll not run into any snares. We're seasoned now and live in anticipation of the enemy's next attempt to impede this journey. Our guidebook is in easy reach as we amble along. Someone further ahead spots the next net in the road and the warning trickles back: "Be careful; we're approaching the pitfall, Selfishness, and it's stretch is almost as wide as the path itself."

It comes as no surprise that the enemy has cast Selfishness as a potential snare; after all, its attribute of being concerned with one's own interest above the interest of others, is not that uncommon. The philosophy of *Me First* seems ingrained in the human condition. But as our guidebook points out, a spirit of Selfishness can send us down the road to disaster. The apostle James writes, *"For where you have envy and selfish ambition, there you will find disorder and every evil practice."*

(James 3:16) Is that not what befell the brothers, Cain and Abel, in the early chapters of the book of Genesis? *"Then the Lord said to Cain, 'Where is your brother, Abel?' 'I don't know,' he replied. 'Am I my brother's keeper?'"* (Genesis 4:9) Cain's envy of his brother and concern for his own interest allowed a seed of jealousy to grow and sprout murder and lies. A brother's selfish ambition pushed him into a snare that resulted in disgrace and exile.

The guidebook further highlights the danger of Selfishness in chapter twenty-five of the first book of Samuel. It tells the story of David, Nabal, and Abagail. During a time when David and his men were in the desert, they had extended protection during the shearing season to the shepherds and sheep belonging to Nabal, who was very wealthy. Sometime later when Nabal was again shearing his sheep, David sent greetings. He asked Nabal to show favorable hospitality toward the men and himself since they had come at a festive time. And he reminded him of the protection he and his men had extended before.

Nabal's response was the ultimate expression of Selfishness. *"Who is this David?... Why should I take my bread and water, and the meat I have slaughtered for my shearers, and give it to men coming from who knows where?"* Despite his wife's intervention that halted David's vengeance, the story did not end well for Nabal. Upon hearing from her what had almost happened as a result of his Selfishness, he suffered heart failure and as scripture records, *"About ten days later, the Lord struck Nabal and he died."* Additional warnings against this attitudinal snare are sprinkled throughout our guidebook. Paul teaches in Philippians 2:3-4 that we are to *"Do nothing out of selfish ambition or vain conceit, but in humility consider others better than yourself. Each of you should look not only to your own interests, but also to the interests of others."* In his letter to the church in Galatia, he includes among the acts of a sinful nature, *"selfish ambition."* (Galatians 5:20)

Some years ago, the American minister and author Robert Fulghum wrote the book, *All I Really Need to Know I Learned in Kindergarten*. Leading the list of those things he learned in that simple and innocent setting is the antithesis of Selfishness. He learned to share; and to put into practice the unselfishness that grows from sharing. One of the more familiar examples of this concept is found in the parable of the Good Samaritan. (Luke 10:30-37) Most of us know the story of how the least likely person to have done so, showed mercy to a traveler left injured alongside the road. Unlike the priest and Levite who passed by, concerned with their own interests and looking out for themselves, the Samaritan shrugged off Selfishness to share both his time and resources to aid the stranger.

Armed with these scriptures, we step carefully along the perimeter of the pitfall. As it recedes from sight, we recall another reference from the guidebook, perhaps the greatest demonstration of selflessness recorded therein: John 3:16. There the apostle John writes, *"God so loved the world that he gave his one and only Son, that whoever believes in him shall not perish but have eternal life."* Given humankind's proclivity toward sin, God could have allowed His creation to self-destruct. But He showed us with the sacrifice of His only son what putting aside one's own interest in favor of another's looks like. He shared Jesus with us. He didn't have to, but He understood that selflessness involves loving; loving that shares what is yours with others.

Reflection

How would you rate yourself on a Selfishness scale of one to ten, with ten representing total self-interest and zero interest or concern for others? Are you a *Me First* person, more inclined to satisfy your needs, before you look to the needs of others?

Day 39

Disappointment

Then you will know that I am the Lord; those who hope in me will not be disappointed.

Isaiah 49:23

Dawn breaks and we move out, trusting our guidebook for guidance to combat whatever snare the enemy has in store today. It's hard to imagine what that might be, as we've already encountered so many pitfalls on this path to glory. Yet scripture reminds us of the devil's stealth: *"Your enemy the devil prowls around like a roaring lion looking for someone to devour."* (1 Peter 5:8) All too soon we recognize what such sneakiness looks like as the next pitfall comes into view. On the surface, Disappointment might not appear to be a snare, but if its spirit is allowed to linger, it can grow into disillusionment and embitterment, two stones believers can easily stumble over, pushing them off the path into the pit.

When David wrote of his forefathers' faith in God— *"They cried to you and were saved; in you they trusted and were not disappointed."* (Psalm 22:4-5)—he was undoubtedly recalling the stories of those before him who had experienced the snare of Disappointment. Feelings of sadness or regret produced by circumstances that frustrate one's hopes, dreams, and expectations are common to the human experience. Our guidebook abounds with such accounts in the lives of some of our biblical ancestors. During a time and in a culture, that equated a woman's value with her ability to bear children, the greatest Disappointment a wife could face was childlessness. This was the case with Sarah, Hannah, and Elizabeth, all married, but without children for many years. Instead, they suffered the bitter taste of barrenness and seasons shrouded in sadness as their prayers for children remained unanswered. When the prophet Elijah's Mount Carmel experience brought not a great revival of faith in God's power as he expected, but a death threat from the queen, his Disappointment was such that he wished for death. It isn't difficult to understand the Disappointment the patriarch Jacob must have felt, when after completing his seven-year work agreement for the right to marry his beloved Rachel, he was tricked into marrying her sister instead. And to rub salt into the wound of that regret, he had to spend another seven years in service before finally marrying her.

Disappointment is ageless. Just as our forebearers knew its pangs, we too grapple with dashed aspirations, betrayed relationships, and unexpected twists of fate that push us to the brink of despair. Just ask the star athlete with a full scholarship who suffers an injury in the last game of the season that kills the dream of college; or the faithful wife and mother who discovers her spouse's betrayal of their marriage vows; or the hard working, dedicated worker next in line for the promotion, listening as it goes instead to the underqualified nephew of the boss; or anyone whose hopes and dreams never materialize and for whom the joys of life remain just out of reach. Such is Disappointment's snare. Giving up or growing weary or believing that things will never change is the loop-hole the enemy seeks to exploit and use to force us into its pit.

A look backward at our aforementioned biblical ancestors who faced down the snare of Disappointment with prayer and faith in God's plans helps as we draw nearer its tentacles. We open our guidebook to God's promises. There we discover the assurances that counter Disappointment. The Apostle John writes, *"If you remain in me and my words remain in you, ask whatever you wish, and it will be given to you"* (John 15:7). We are reminded in the words of Paul that God is able to do for us *"immeasurably more than all we ask or imagine, according to his work within us."* (Ephesians 3:20). And in his personal testimony of dealing with life's inevitable seasons of Disappointment, Paul writes, *"... for I have learned to be content whatever the circumstances... I can do everything through him who gives me strength."* (Philippians 4:11-13). Finally, the writer of Hebrews captures the essence of God's promises when Disappointment threatens: *"God has said, 'Never will I leave you; never will I forsake you.' So, we say with confidence, 'the Lord is my helper; I will not be afraid. What can man do to me?'"* (Hebrews 13:5-6). Yes, disappointing experiences can send us into a tailspin, away from the path to our ultimate destination. But with God's word as the source of our strength and our guide, we can navigate around this pitfall and continue the journey in faith.

Reflection

What are your thoughts regarding this pitfall? Do you see Disappointment as a threat to a believer's faith journey? What have been some of your most Disappointing experiences? Was your faith shaken, or strengthened during that time?

Day 40

CYNICISM

Why did you bring the Lord's community into this desert?
Why did you bring us up out of Egypt to this terrible place?
                                        Numbers 20:4-5

For some time now, we've been on this road to glory; our passage marked by one encounter after another with pitfalls lining the path. The relentlessness of the enemy to deter us weighs heavily upon some of our fellow believers. We hear their occasional murmurs of negativity grow louder and more frequent. Eventually someone asks, "How certain are we that this road to eternity is worth all the trials and tribulations we continue to experience? Shouldn't we be spared them since we've committed to following the Savior? Why are we always on the lookout for another snare?"

Another voice rises. "Yes, those are valid questions. In light of the ongoing pitfalls we're encountering, I'm beginning to question if this journey will end as we hope it will." Above a collective gasp of astonishment at these seemingly captious comments, one of the faithful heralds, "I think I know what pitfall awaits us next on the path: Cynicism."

The dictionary defines Cynicism as skepticism,

distrustfulness of human nature and motives, suspicious, derisive, mocking, and generally believing people are motivated purely by their own selfish interests. Early in our biblical history we see Cynicism continually taint the spirit of God's people, irrespective of His divine interventions on their behalf. With ample evidence to the contrary, they were skeptical of all Moses did under God's direction to lead them out of slavery into the promised land. Each bump in the road revealed their distrust of Moses' motives and ultimately of God's plans for them; despite the miracle God had performed in their Red Sea crossing.

As they journeyed following this divine deliverance, we hear their Cynicism as they confronted Moses and Aaron time and time again. *"Is it because there were no graves in Egypt that you have taken us away to die in the wilderness?"* (Exodus 4:11-12) *"If only we had died by the Lord's hand in Egypt!"* (Exodus 16:3)

For a moment, Cynicism touched even Job, the man we revere for his example of sinless suffering. Though God said of him: *"Have you considered my servant Job? There is no one on earth like him; he is blameless and upright, a man who fears God and shuns evil,"* Job yielded in cynical questioning of what had befallen him. *"Why is light given to those in misery, and life to the bitter of soul? Why is life given to a man whose way is hidden, whom God has hedged in?"* (Job 1:8; 3:20-23) And as he continued to seek the meaning of his tragedies, Cynicism had its way. Its snare lay at the heart of the questions he put to God: *"Why did you bring me out of the womb? If only I had never come into being or had been carried straight from the womb to the grave!"* (Job 10:18-19) *"I loathe my very life; … Does it please you to oppress me, to spurn the work of your hands, while you smile on the schemes of the wicked?"* (Job 10:1-3)

And was it not skepticism and distrust of God's motives that caused the prophet Jeremiah to complain, *"O, Lord, you deceived me." "Cursed be the day I was born!" "Why did I ever come out of the womb to see trouble and sorrow and to end my days in shame?"* (Jeremiah 20:7, 14, 18) Cynicism is a powerful force whose net of negativity and distrust can snare anyone. Biblical stories such as these show us that Cynicism is not new. It has threatened man's relationship with God from the beginning. It feeds upon the spirit when the circumstances of life crush, overwhelm, disappoint, or fail to meet expectations. Those we look to for leadership and direction don't just fail to deliver, but more alarmingly seem not to care. Those of younger generations look at their elders and see hypocrisy and deceit; unmerited suffering; unending violence and war; and pursuit of whatever is expedient and increases the gap between the rich and the poor. Whether within or outside our spheres of influence, these conditions spawn the skepticism and distrust which can send us tumbling into the Cynicism pitfall.

What seems common sense rationale for Cynicism in the climate of our times is only avoided by the encouragement we find in our guidebook. In these scriptures that are God-breathed, we find what we need to avoid the pitfall: *"Rejoice in the Lord always. Do not be anxious about anything, but in everything, by prayer and petition, with thanksgiving, present your requests to God. Whatever is true, whatever is noble, whatever is right, whatever is pure, think about these things."* (Philippians 4:4-8) *"Do not repay evil with evil or insult with insult. On the contrary, repay evil with blessing."* (1 Peter 3:9) *"The Lord is not slow in keeping His promise, as some understand slowness. Instead He is patient with you, not wanting anyone to perish, but everyone to come to repentance."* (2 Peter 3:9) *"And we know that in all things God works for the good of those who love Him, who have been called according to His purpose."* (Romans 8:28)

Armed with these biblical inoculators against Cynicism's minions of distrust, negativity, skepticism, suspicion, and disbelief, the faithful continue, sidestepping yet another snare. And with greater confidence they can stay the course.

Reflection

On a scale of one to ten, with ten representing absolute Cynicism, where do you rank? What circumstances raise your Cynicism? Overall, do you look at life with a cynical lens or a more rose-colored one? If this is a pitfall with which you struggle, what strategies can you adopt to fight its influence? Begin to journal your efforts in this regard.

A Final Word

Your word is a lamp to my feet and a light for my path.
Psalm 119:105

"PARADISE FOUND" read the banner on the cover of a popular home décor magazine that sells outdoor living furniture. It proffered *Paradise* as something available in the here and now in one's own backyard, if of course you can afford the cost of the furnishings. But we believers on this journey know better. Paradise is Heaven, our ultimate destination, not some island resort or backyard filled with island furnishings. Reaching the place where true and lasting treasures will be ours has been our goal since we set upon our quest. Like the treasure hunters referenced in the introduction, we discovered the enemy's relentless attempts to snare us as we made our way upon the path. (Psalm 142:3)

But unlike the juxtaposed treasure seekers, we should not have been surprised by the pitfalls we encountered along the way. In fact, the many biblical references to the path and its implications for believers were in our guidebook, shining a light for all who would but take the time to read them. The psalmist wrote, *"Teach me your way, O Lord; lead me in a straight path because of my oppressors."* (Psalm 27:11) In Psalm 16:11, he declared, *"You have made known to me the path of life."* And in an affirmation of God's power to protect him, David penned, *"But my eyes are fixed on you, O Sovereign Lord; in you I take refuge—do not give me over to death. Keep me from the snares they have laid for me, from the traps set by evildoers. Let the wicked fall into their own nets, while I pass by in safety."* (Psalm 142:8-10)

Perhaps the best summation of the perils on the path to paradise is found in Jesus' Parable of the Sower. (Luke 8:11-12) The sown seed is the word of God heard by those who are on the path; it is the reason for their journey. But as the preceding chapters have shown, hearing the word is not enough. The devil's snares dot the landscape; they represent the human conditions that enable him to *"take away the word from their hearts, so that they may not believe and be saved."*

Other snares entangle those on the path who receive the word joyfully, but who yield to the inevitable trials that test their faith. Still others on this road to glory fall prey to the pitfalls caused by *"life's worries, riches and pleasures"* that prevent their maturity in the faith. Heavenly paradise awaits those whom Jesus describes as *"good soil."* They are the believers on the path who not only hear the word but retain it; who persevere because the truth of God's word gives them the guidance, direction, and strength they need to stay the course, helped by God at every turn.

When we trust in the Lord with all our hearts and lean not on our understanding; and acknowledge Him in all our ways, He will make the path straight. (Proverbs 3:5-6) And if we do fall, God Himself will draw us up out of the horrible pit of tumult and destruction, out of the miry clay, froth and slime, and set our feet once again on the path with steady steps that establish our journey. (Psalm 40:2)

To God be the glory!

Reflection

As you end this forty-day devotional experience, what has kept you reading? Did the chapters speak to your personal journey? What is your biggest take away as you stay the course on your journey to Heaven?

Acknowledgements

Be joyful always; pray continually; give thanks in all circumstances, for this is God's will for you in Christ Jesus.
1 Thessalonians 5:16-18

The writing of this third book has been led by the Holy Spirit and inspired by the word of God as contained in Holy Scripture. I began writing it as soon as my second book was on its way to publication. It seemed almost effortless on my part; as always, I felt prompted by the Savior with the words to pen. Some days the word flow was unnerving. But I need to be clear. I can take no credit for the resultant effort. All credit goes to the Lord for His mercy, grace, and favor in using me to bring a word of hope and encouragement to those who will read this book. I shall be forever grateful to my Lord and Savior for the gift of devotional wordsmithing He bestowed. And as long as He so allows, I shall use it to His glory.

Truly I could not have finished this project without the love and support of my sister in Christ and forever friend,

Ann Lloyd. She was my *critical ear* throughout the months of writing. With such an ear, she listened to each piece; offering from her perspective as a long time Bible study teacher and lay leader, what I might need to refine the message of each chapter. I am indebted to her; and thankful for her insight and continuing words of encouragement. We make a great team.

I also thank my family and friends who have been so supportive of my current book, *Sonshine: Reflections of Faith*, that I published in August 2017. They have further encouraged me with their positive feedback and wanting me to write another. Just yesterday (the first Sunday of January 2018), a friend and church member came over to ask if I was working on another book and to share that she had finished *Sonshine* but was rereading it to begin the new year as she waits on the next one to be published. To God be the glory.

Finally, I am thankful to WordCrafts Press and Mike Parker for seeing merit in this book and undertaking its publication.

Beverly ND Clopton

Also Available From

Beverly ND Clopton

Sonshine:
  Reflections of Faith

Heaven or Bust
  Journey to Glory

Also Available From

WordCrafts Press

Pressing Foward
  by April Poynter

Morning Mist: *Stories from the Water's Edge*
  by Barbie Loflin

Youth Ministry is Easy! *and 9 other lies*
  by Aaron Shaver

Chronicles of a Believer
  by Don McCain

Illuminations
  by Paula K. Parker & Tracy Sugg

A Scarlet Cord of Hope
  by Sheryl Griffin

www.wordcrafts.net

www.ingramcontent.com/pod-product-compliance
Lightning Source LLC
Chambersburg PA
CBHW052140110526
44591CB00012B/1799